Fantasmagoria

A New Burlington Book
Conceived, edited, and designed by Marshall Editions
The Old Brewery, 6 Blundell Street, London N7 9BH, UK
www.quarto.com

Copyright © 2009 Marshall Editions

Publisher: Jenni Johns
Commissioning editor: Claudia Martin
Art director: Ivo Marloh
Layout: 3rd-i, Vanessa Green, Cecilia Bandiera
Managing editor: Paul Docherty
Project editor: Amy Head
Picture manager: Veneta Bullen
Indexer: Vicki Robinson
Production: Nikki Ingram

ISBN 10: 1-84566-326-8
ISBN 13: 978-1-84566-326-1

Printed and bound in Singapore by Star Standard Industries (Pte) Ltd

10 9 8 7 6 5 4 3 2 1

Fantasmagoria

An Atlas of Fabulous Creatures, Enchanted Beings, and Magical Monsters

Julia Bruce

TABLE OF CONTENTS

Introduction 6

Chapter 1:
Fairies and the Little People 8

Fairies and Pixies 10
Fairies' Tales 12
Elves.. 14
Brownies 16
Boggarts 18
Goblins 20
Gremlins 22
Dwarves 24
Gnomes.. 26

Chapter 2:
Wonder Workers 28

Witches 30
Witches on Trial 32
Wizards and Magicians............................ 34
Famous Wizards....................................... 36
Djinn... 38
Spiritualists 40
Shamans... 42

Chapter 3:
Evil Sprits, Demons, and the Undead....................... 44

Vampires 46
Mummies... 48

Zombies and Golems............................... 50
Ghosts.. 52
Deathly Spirits... 54
Demons.. 56

Chapter 4:
Humanoid Creatures 58

Werewolves 60
Yeti and Sasquatch 62
Giants... 66
Monstrous Women 68
Men of Wood and Forest......................... 70

Chapter 5:
Horned and Hoofed Creatures...... 72

Unicorns 74
Pegasus... 76
Water Horses.. 78
The Minotaur 80
Centaurs 82
Satyrs 84

Chapter 6:
Dragons 86

Dragon Lore 88
Chinese Dragons 90
Japanese Dragons 92
Greek Dragons 94
Dragon Slayers 96

Chapter 7:

Four-legged Fiends 98

Vampire Cats 100
The Griffin 102
Sphinx 104
Ammut 106
Cerubus 108
Black Dogs and Death Hounds 110

Chapter 8:

Fabulous Birds 112

The Phoenix 114
The Thunderbird 116
The Roc 118
The Simurgh 120
Feathered Fiends 122

Chapter 9:

Water Creatures 124

Mermaids 126
Nixes and Nymphs 128
Scylla and Charybdis 130
Lake Lurkers 132
Monsters of the Deep 134
River Monsters 136

Glossary 138
Further Reading 140
Index 141
Acknowledgments 144

INTRODUCTION

Here be dragons … and vampires, fairies, elves, ghosts, werewolves, witches, wizards, and all manner of monsters and men. Fantastic creatures, supernatural powers, and tales of gods and men have fascinated people all across the world for thousands of years. In these pages you will meet some of the world's most amazing creatures: some humanoid, some god-like, and some thoroughly devilish.

This journey is not, however, for the faint-hearted. Be prepared for some truly terrifying creatures, terrible stories, and fantastical facts. There is a smattering of the weird and wonderful, too, and even the downright ridiculous. Did you know, for example, that to flatter the Chinese Emperor the best thing you could do was call him "Dragon Face," and that in Morocco there is a djinni, or genie, that haunts toilets? You'll also find some practical advice, such as why you should be careful when approaching water in northern England, how to deal with werewolves, how to tell if someone has been possessed by a demon, and what to do if a mischievous boggart invades your home.

Each chapter begins with a map, showing the locations of some of the more notable beings. You will also find at the back of the book a glossary, suggestions for further reading, and some interesting websites where you can continue your research.

Enjoy your journey, and do take care …

Fairies and the Little People

Many of us have grown up with the idea that fairies are pretty, tiny, winged creatures that scatter fairy dust, dance round fairy rings, and have names like Tinker Bell. The truth can be a lot more sinister. There are tales of fairy folk who are as big as humans and think nothing of abducting people or using them for their own ends. Others are far from beautiful, such as the hideous fairy Melusine. There are also mischievous little people and household spirits in almost every culture, who can be helpful to the people they live with but might also make trouble if they are crossed. From the nisse of Scandinavia to the domovoi of Russia, the ein saung nat of Burma, and the brownie of Scotland, not to mention boggarts, gremlins, and goblins: all of these little monsters can be very difficult to live with!

North America

Atlantic Ocean

South America

❶ England
Troublemaking boggarts, mischievous Cornish pixies, elves, goblins, gremlins, gnomes

❷ Ireland
Leprechauns, elves

❸ Scotland
Brownies, helpful household spirits

❹ Scandinavia
Underground-dwelling dwarves, nisse, elves, vættir

❺ Persia (Iran)
The beautiful peri

❻ India
The wise and mysterious vidyeshvaras

❼ Philippines
The tree-dwelling diwata

❽ Benin
Aziza, the forest fairies

❾ New Zealand
The patupairehe

❿ North America
Elves, fairies, gremlins

⓫ Burma
The ein saung nat

⓬ Russia/Eastern Europe
The hearth-dwelling domovoi

⓭ Pyrenees
The Goblins

⓮ Germany
Gnomes, dwarves, and the vicious erlkings

⓯ Tibet
The nang-lha, room-shifting household spirit

⓰ Alps
The bearded barbegazi, gnomes of the snow

⓱ France
Serpent-tailed Melusine

Arctic Ocean

N
W · E
S

Europe

①② ③ ④
⑭ ⑯
⑰
⑬

⑫

Asia

⑤

⑮

⑥ ⑪

Pacific Ocean

Africa

⑧

Indian Ocean

Australia

⑨

FAIRIES AND PIXIES

Welcome to the world of the little people. Fairies are the enchanted beings that have given their name to "fairy tales"—all manner of stories about strange creatures and magical happenings. However, things that happen in fairy tales are not always good and neither are fairies ….

Above *The common image of fairies as tiny, winged beings probably comes from Persian stories about peri—small, magical creatures that had once been angels.*

When you think about fairies you might imagine tiny creatures with gossamer wings flitting between flowers and scattering fairy dust in their wake. You might think of Peter Pan's Tinker Bell or the Blue Fairy in Pinocchio. But these are very modern ideas of fairies. In the dim and distant past fairies were not always good, cute, or beautiful, or even small!

In some of the oldest stories fairies were the same size as people—not quite spirits but not quite human either. They had magical powers and a deep connection with nature. Some were tall, bright, and beautiful; others were dark and ugly like trolls. Most were invisible unless they chose to show themselves, and some, such as the terrifying Melusine, could even shape-shift.

Other tales described fairies as angels who had argued with God and were locked out of heaven, doomed to roam the Earth forever. In British, Irish, and European folktales, fairies are magical little beings, sometimes good and sometimes wicked, that live in woodland, in meadows, or underground. We can't be sure of the truth, but one thing is for certain: people have to be careful around fairies, because although they can be kind, if they are upset they can do a lot of harm. Fairies have been accused of horrible acts, such as beating travelers, stealing children, and causing wasting illnesses, paralysis, and even death!

WORLD FAIRIES

You will find stories of fairy people all over the world, and in all places fairies have a deep connection with nature. In India, fairies are called vidyeshvaras. They are secretive beings who guard forests and wild places.

The Maori people of New Zealand tell tales of the patupairehe—white-skinned, red-haired spirits of mists and forests who love music and dancing. Although they might teach you some magic if you can find them, it's more likely that their beautiful music will lead you deep into the forest until you are hopelessly lost. In Persia (modern-day Iran) peri are beautiful fairy people of forests and rivers and are kindly towards humans. Equally beautiful are the diwata who live in trees in the Philippines and curse anyone who harms the forest. The aziza of Benin, in Africa, are also forest fairies—they use their fairy magic to help human hunters.

Above On certain days, the fairy Melusine turned into a water serpent from the waist down. Amazingly, she managed to hide this from her husband for many years, but when he eventually found her out she turned herself into a dragon and disappeared.

PIXIES

In the southwest of England lives a band of fairies called pixies, or piskies. Pixies are small, wingless, and usually red-haired. They have pointed ears and wear green clothes and pointy hats. Fun-loving and mischievous, pixies like to dance and play and will lure children to join in. They are usually kind to humans, especially anyone who needs help around the house, but they sometimes play tricks on people, perhaps by stealing their belongings or leading them astray. Pixies love horses and will often steal them and ride wildly round and round in circles. This circular movement forms a fairy ring, or gallitrap. Anyone who dares to step inside a gallitrap takes their life in their hands, as they will fall under the power of the pixies.

Below This picture, from the early 20th century, shows pixies as fun-loving and faintly comical little people, here on their way to a carnival.

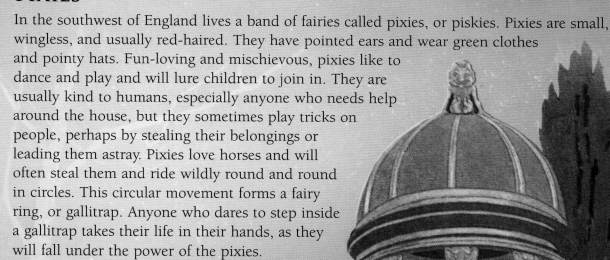

WINGED FAIRIES

Of all the little people, the best known are the winged fairies, who can be found in legends and fables all over the world. Winged fairies are usually depicted as small, pretty, and charming. But they can also be spiteful if people get on the wrong side of them.

LUSMORE AND THE FAIRIES

A long time ago in the midlands of Ireland, there was a poor humpbacked man who earned a living by plaiting straw and rushes into hats and baskets. The local people called the man Lusmore, because he wore a sprig of lusmore, or foxglove, in his straw hat.

One night, Lusmore was walking home when he came to the old, crumbling castle of Knockgrafton, a wild and magical place. Feeling weary, he rested beside the castle moat, its water silver under the moon. Just then he heard notes of strange, unearthly music, like the sound of many voices blended together. The words of the song were repeated again and again, and Lusmore listened so carefully that after a while he was able to join in. The song was being sung by fairies, who, when they heard Lusmore's melodic voice, were

Right Oberon and Titania, king and queen of the fairies, meet in the dark woods in this painting by Arthur Rackham.

delighted. The fairies surrounded Lusmore, and one of them stepped forward and chanted the words: "Lusmore, Lusmore! Doubt not, nor deplore. For the hump which you bore on your back is no more. Look down on the floor, and view it, Lusmore!"

On hearing these words, Lusmore felt himself becoming strangely happy and— miraculously—he saw his hump tumbling down from his back to the ground. So great was his ecstasy that he fell into a sound sleep. When he awoke he found himself beside the moat, in brilliant sunshine. When he nervously touched his back to feel his hump he found it was gone!

Lusmore went back to his village and carried on patiently plaiting his straw into hats and baskets. But the story of how he lost his hump spread far and wide. It even reached as far as Waterford, in the southeast of Ireland, where there lived a mean-spirited and cunning humpback named Jack Madden. Soon enough, Jack Madden made his way to Knockgrafton. When he heard the fairy music, instead of listening carefully and adding to the harmonious sounds, he impatiently joined in, out of tune and out of time. In a flash, the fairies crowded around Jack. One of them chanted at him: "Jack Madden, Jack Madden! Your words came so bad in the tune we felt glad in, that your life we may sadden; here's two humps for Jack Madden!" Sure enough, in an instant, Jack found himself with two humps on his back—his own and Lusmore's old one.

THE COTTINGLEY FAIRIES

In the early 1900s, two young cousins named Frances Griffiths and Elsie Wright claimed they had taken photographs of fairies at Elsie's home in Cottingley, near Bradford, England. The photos showed creatures that looked like miniature humans with large wings. They were dressed in filmy clothes. Many people, including the writer Sir Arthur Conan Doyle, author of the Sherlock Holmes stories, believed that the photos proved the existence of fairies. In the 1970s, however, it was shown that the fairies were in fact pictures that had been cut out from a book. Even so, Frances Griffiths continued to insist until her death that one of the photos was genuine.

Above Frances Griffiths and a winged fairy.

Opposite Hunchback Lusmore charmed the fairies of the Knockgrafton Castle with his sweet singing.

ELVES

People have been telling stories about elves for over 2,000 years. Elves are often shown as human-sized beings, beautiful, magical, and immortal, who live in harmony with nature. But small, mischievous elves also appear in the folk stories of many countries.

Above *The elves of popular English folklore are tiny people, who live at one with nature and are often mischievous.*

Elves first appear in the myths of the Norse people, who lived in Sweden, Norway, Denmark, and Iceland over a thousand years ago. They said that elves were the spirits of the dead. In Icelandic tales there were good and beautiful light elves, who lived in the sky, and wicked and ugly dark elves, who lived underground. The dark elves were born from maggots that fed on the corpse of a giant called Ymir.

Other stories described elves as beautiful women who lived in the forest. But if you looked at them from a certain angle, you would see that they were hollow! Elves could enchant humans, luring mortal men into fairy rings or making them join their wild dances until they dropped dead from exhaustion. Anyone unlucky enough to see elves dancing would find that while they had been watching, many years had passed in the real world.

TINY ELFIN FOLK

English stories often show elves as mischievous beings that cause trouble for people who annoy them. They are tiny folk with pointed ears and comical red hats. In North America, England, and Ireland, elves are also little people who help Santa Claus make Christmas toys for children in his workshop at the North Pole.

Right The elves in J.R.R. Tolkien's famous books The Hobbit *and* The Lord of the Rings *are magically gifted beings, as large as humans but wiser and more beautiful, with sharper senses. They have delicate features and pointed ears.*

Above *Early descriptions of leprechauns have them wearing red as well as green.*

LEPRECHAUNS

Leprechauns are merry shoemakers who live in Ireland. It is said that you can hear their tap, tap, tapping as they make shoes for fairies. These little elves usually wear green outfits, with large metal buckles on their shoes and tall black hats. Leprechauns are thought to hoard pots of gold, which they might give to you if you are lucky. If you do catch one, make sure you keep him in your sights. If you take your eyes off him for even a second, the leprechaun will vanish into thin air.

15

BROWNIES

Brownies are household spirits, who do chores at night while humans sleep. They don't like to be seen so they hide during the day. They are known by different names in different countries: brownies in Scotland, for instance, hobs in northern England, Heinzelmännchen in Germany and nisse in Scandinavia.

Below *A household brownie enjoys his supper of a bowl of milk. Keeping your brownie well fed is a sure way to keep in his good books so that he will protect your house.*

Do's and don'ts

- **Do** thank your brownie by leaving small gifts of food.
- **Do** leave porridge and butter, cream, milk, and honey.
- **Don't** offer money to your brownie.
- **Don't** whistle or swear where your brownie can hear you.
- **Don't** change anything that your brownie likes.
- **Don't** insult your brownie.

It is said that you are very lucky if you have a brownie in your house. But people should be warned—if they upset a brownie, they could lose him for good. Brownies like to be left tidbits of food as thanks for their hard work—particular favorites are milk, cream, honey, and porridge. However, if they think these gifts are payments, they will feel insulted and will probably leave the house or begin to cause all kinds of mischief instead.

Usually, only people with the gift of second sight can see brownies, although they can make themselves visible to people if they wish. They look like little men, no taller than a small child. They have long hair and usually wear a brown cloak or a blue hat.

NISSE OF THE NORTH

In Sweden and Norway household spirits are called nisse or tomte. They protect farmers and their families and animals, especially at night. Nisse particularly like horses and will groom their favorite horse and braid its mane and tail. Like brownies nisse are small, but even so they are very strong. Also like brownies they can be very touchy, and they don't like change. If they are disturbed or feel they have been insulted, they are likely to cause trouble and mischief, perhaps by breaking things or tying cows' tails together! To keep a nisse happy, make sure he always has his favorite food—porridge with butter.

Left In Burma (Myanmar) spirits like the one this statue represents are called nats. The ein saung nat is the guardian of the home.

Above No Russian home is complete without its own bearded domovoi. Beware—an angry domovoi is dangerous!

DOMOVOI

In Russia, every home is said to have a domovoi—a house sprite who looks like a little old man with a grey beard and lives behind the stove. Like the brownie, a domovoi guards the house and its inhabitants and sometimes helps with household chores or works on the farm. To attract a domovoi to a new house you should put on your best clothes, stand outside your house, and shout, "Dedushka Dobrokhot, please come into my house and tend the flocks," or put some bread under the stove to coax one in. A friendly domovoi can warn his household of danger or predict good things, such as a wedding or a good harvest. But beware the unhappy domovoi. He can cause havoc by moving or breaking objects, moaning, and banging. A very angry domovoi might go so far as to suffocate people in their beds or even burn down the house!

BOGGARTS

Unlike brownies, who generally do good deeds, boggarts are wicked household spirits. They are sly and mischievous hobgoblins who play mean tricks, such as rearranging furniture, pulling bedsheets off unwary sleepers, making things disappear, turning milk sour, and making animals lame. Once you have a boggart, you'll never get rid of it!

Below   In the Harry Potter books by J.K. Rowling, boggarts are shape-shifters that can take on the form of the viewer's worst fear. To counter this power, the victim should think hard about something that will make the boggart look ridiculous. Here, a boggart approaches in the form of Harry's greatest fear, a dementor.

Do's and don'ts

- **Do** leave the best food for your boggart to keep him happy.

- **Don't** anger your boggart by insulting him or trying to trick him.

- **Don't** try to leave your boggart behind; he will just follow you.

Boggarts flitting

There was once an honest farmer in whose house a boggart had taken up residence. The pesky creature tormented the farmer's children mercilessly. It snatched their food, knocked over their milk, pulled at their bedcurtains, and sat on their chests as they slept. On hearing their children's cries, the farmer and his wife would rush to their aid, but the boggart was sly and made sure he was never seen.

Eventually, the farmer and his family could stand the wretched creature and his mischievous ways no longer. The farmer gathered all his belongings and his wife and children and piled them all into his cart. When his neighbor saw what he was doing he asked if he was leaving at last. The farmer replied that yes, he was flitting, as he could see no other way to escape the wicked boggart. But no sooner were the words out of his mouth than a voice piped up from the back of the cart, "Ay, we're flitting, ye see!" It was the boggart, ready to go with them to their new house. Defeated, the farmer told his wife they may as well unpack and go back to the old house, boggart and all. Better to be plagued by it at home than in another house that was less familiar!

Chamber Hall boggart

Chamber Hall in Oldham, northern England, was plagued by a boggart for many years. Every night, the inhabitants would leave food to satisfy it, but one night a new maid was tempted by the delicious tidbits she should have left for the creature and ate them herself, saying that plain churn milk and barley bread was good enough for the boggart. She finished her ironing and went to bed. Later that night, the whole house was awakened by her screams. The boggart had branded her with her own iron, chanting "Churn milk and barley bread" as he did so. Eventually the boggart was driven from the house, but mysterious noises and knockings can still be heard now and again in the dead of night, and locals reckon the boggart sits brooding in a thorn tree just down the road from the house. Perhaps he hasn't really left, after all.

Right In his book Ouselwood, James Dronsfield told the story of the Chamber Hall boggart. The intruder was said to have been buried beneath the doorstone of the house. But did it escape?

GOBLINS

Evil, mischievous, ugly, bad-tempered—folktales have very few good things to say about goblins. According to legend these small, gnome-like troublemakers came from the Pyrenees mountains between France and Spain. From there they pinched, prodded, and scared their way across Europe, eventually finding their way to Britain and beyond.

Goblins wander from place to place and do not have proper homes. They usually live in dead trees, holes, and caves, but sometimes might come to live in a human's house. If they do, they will frighten the animals, pester the people, and generally cause trouble. It is said that a goblin's smile can curdle the blood and that its laugh will turn milk sour. Although these goblins are naughty, they don't cause any real harm. But there are other, very scary types of goblin, such as the terrifying erlkings, written about in German stories. They use strange visions to lure people, especially children, to their deaths!

NANG-LHA

High up in the Himalayan mountains you will find the land of Tibet. Here, many homes have a nang-lha, a god or spirit that

Left In folkstories, many unlucky householders suffer sleepless nights at the hands of goblins, who come out at night to play their tricks and generally wreak havoc.

CAU'D LAD OF HYLTON

In County Durham—now Tyne and Wear—in the northeast of England, a goblin called the Cau'd Lad of Hylton plagued the residents of Hylton Castle every night with his wicked pranks. He was heard to cry out "I'm cau'd!" ("I'm cold!"), so in desperation one evening, the maids left him a warm, green cloak. When he saw the cloak, the little man danced with delight, wrapped it around himself, and disappeared through a window, never to trouble the castle again.

But this mischief-maker didn't stop with household tricks. According to one story, the Cau'd Lad sometimes ventured out of the castle and posed as a ferryman on the River Wear. He would take passengers halfway across the river and then leave them stranded there!

Above *The Cau'd Lad of Hylton Castle cavorts with glee at the sight of the warm cloak left out for him.*

protects the house. The nang-lha are quite scary to look at. They have a body like that of a man but the head of a pig or a wild boar, and they wear long, flowing robes. In their right hand this spirit carries a three-pronged stick made out of a poisonous wood.

The nang-lha lives in different parts of the house at different times of year, and he is very strict. For instance, when he is in a particular part of the house, people are not allowed to go there and it must not be cleaned or disturbed in any way. If he is in the center of the house where the fire is, the grate must be moved. When he moves to a doorway, no bride, groom, or dead body may pass through. But as long as his rules are followed and he is properly looked after (with gifts of tea or beer), the nang-lha will guard the house and all who live in it.

Tibetan household gods are believed to be the spirits of family ancestors. When the seasons change, it is traditional for families to hold special ceremonies to honor them.

GREMLINS

Almost 100 years ago, the world was plunged into a terrible war. Now known as World War One (1914–1918) this was the first war that used airplanes in battle. At the same time, a new type of mischievous creature made its first appearance, causing mechanical problems in fighter aircraft. These troublesome sprites soon became known as gremlins.

Above *Gremlins first appeared as meddlesome monsters on fighter planes during the two World Wars.*

MODERN MONSTERS

These days, gremlins like to get into anything mechanical or electronic, not just planes. Unexplained technical glitches are often explained away by their meddling—cars and computers are particular favorites for attack. In the 1980s, stories of gremlins inspired the children's films *Gremlins* and *Gremlins II*, where they are shown as sweet furry creatures who, under the right conditions, turn into grotesque little monsters with sharp teeth and claws and large, bat-like ears. In this form they go on massive destruction sprees. Luckily, these gremlins are only active at night and are destroyed by sunlight.

Above *A gruesome gremlin causes trouble in the children's film* Gremlins, *released in 1984.*

Gremlins caused even more trouble for pilots in World War Two (1939–1945). Gremlins love to fly, but unfortunately for them, they have no wings. Perhaps this is why they love planes so much and, once on board, they cannot resist tinkering with the controls. World War Two pilots reported all sorts of unexplained problems with their radios, engines, navigation, and steering, all of which they blamed on gremlins. Some even claimed to have seen these little pests in action. They described them as ugly little men wearing flying jackets and goggles, or old-fashioned hats and cloaks, who lived in holes next to airfields. Gremlins played wicked tricks outside planes, too. It was said they could even move airstrips or rearrange the patterns of stars in the sky so the pilots couldn't navigate. Of course, gremlins found all these tricks and pranks incredibly funny and laughed uncontrollably at the mayhem they caused.

ROALD DAHL, WALT DISNEY, AND GREMLINS

The famous children's author Roald Dahl was a pilot in the British Royal Air Force in World War Two. He had first-hand experience of gremlins when his plane crash-landed in the North African desert and chose them as the subject of his first book, *The Gremlins*, which was published in 1943. A friend suggested he send the story to the film-maker Walt Disney, who loved it and helped get a version of it published. Disney also put stories about gremlins in his comic-book series, *Walt Disney's Comics and Stories*, bringing the idea of these mischievous little monsters to children across the world.

Although Roald Dahl claimed to have coined the name, gremlins were talked and written about long before his 1943 book. Some people say that the name comes from a combination of "Grimm," as in the Brothers Grimm, who wrote a famous collection of fairy tales, and "Fremlins," a popular beer in England during World War One. Others think it comes from the Old English word "gremain," which means to annoy.

DWARVES

Dwarves in fairy tales are small, dark men who mine deep underground for precious metals and stones. But long before these stories, the Norse people told of very different types of dwarves who were as big as mortal men, had pale skin, and were believed to be spirits of the dead.

The earliest stories about dwarves describe them as dark elves. But whereas elves are bright, young, and beautiful, dwarves are old and ugly—but always wise. Dwarves in fairy tales are usually friendly, fun-loving, and enjoy feasting, like the kindly dwarves in Snow White. Miners believed that dwarves were bringers of good luck and told tales of dwarves rapping on mine walls to warn them about rockfalls or floods. However, dwarves are not always good. They sometimes steal, and there are stories of nasty, selfish dwarves such as Rumpelstiltskin and Alberich, the dwarf king.

Do's and don'ts

- **Do** take notice of dwarves' warnings in caves and mines.
- **Do** leave gifts of food and drink if you want to please a dwarf.
- **Don't** swear or whistle when a dwarf is present.

Below *The princess's messenger stumbled across Rumpelstiltskin and overheard him chanting his name.*

RUMPELSTILTSKIN

There was once a proud miller who boasted that his daughter could spin straw into gold. When the king heard of this, he locked the girl up with a pile of straw and a spinning wheel and demanded that for three nights she spin the straw into gold or else he would lock her up forever. Of course, the poor girl could not do it and sat weeping in fear and sorrow. Suddenly, a strange little man appeared. He agreed to spin the straw for her in return for her necklace. The second night he appeared again and again spun the straw into gold, this time in exchange for her ring. But on the third night she had nothing else to offer him, so instead he said he would spin the straw only if she agreed to give him her first-born child. Reluctantly she agreed, and the dwarf spun the straw for the third and final night. Delighted with the gold, the king ordered that the girl should marry his son, the prince. Eventually, the young couple had a child, but as soon as it was born, the dwarf reappeared to claim his payment. Horrified, the girl struck a bargain with him. He would let her keep her babe if she could guess his name in three days. For two days she tried all the names she could think of but couldn't guess it. Then, on the second night, her messenger overheard the dwarf as he hopped about his fire, singing a strange song that ended in his name. So on the third day when the dwarf came to the girl, she was able to reveal his name—Rumpelstiltskin. Furious, the angry dwarf flew out of the room and was never seen again.

ALBERICH—KING OF THE DWARVES

In German legends Alberich was the hideous king of the dwarves. He was a fearful tyrant and was very cruel to his dwarf people, forcing them to work underground digging out precious metals and gems to make him rich and to adorn his magnificent palace. Alberich was also a powerful magician and the guardian of a priceless hoard of stolen gold and a magic ring. One day, the gods Loki and Wotan came across Alberich and saw his gold. They tricked him into turning himself into a toad, then squashed him underfoot and carried off the pilfered gold and the ring. Alberich survived but at a price: he had lost all his gold and power.

Left *Tyrannical Alberich oppressed his people, turning them into his unwilling slaves. He grew very rich off their labor.*

GNOMES

Gnomes are different from other little people of folklore. Only 500 years ago, a doctor called Paracelsus invented their name to describe spirits of the earth, but stories of gnome-like creatures go back much further. Although they are similar, gnomes should not be confused with either goblins or dwarves.

Fantastical fact

Bankers in Switzerland are often called gnomes, because they look after large amounts of money the same way that gnomes guard hoards of gold.

Above *In 1917, a young girl called Frances Griffiths claimed to have taken a photograph of a gnome dancing for her cousin, Elsie Wright.*

Today, gnomes are thought of as pleasant-looking creatures, only about 6 inches (15 cm) tall, with white beards and brightly-colored clothing. Males wear red caps and females wear green. Like dwarves, gnomes will often have a hoard of gold or treasure that they guard closely. As underground-dwellers with special abilities, gnomes can walk through earth as easily as we can walk on top of it. Because sunlight turns them into stone, gnomes only come to the surface at night so you won't often see them, though some people say they can wander above ground in daylight by turning themselves into toads. Gnomes are generally kindly souls. They will always help trapped or injured animals and enjoy gardening and tending plants.

A GNOME BY ANY OTHER NAME

Although the word "gnome" is quite new, stories of gnome-like creatures have been told across Europe for hundreds of years. In medieval times gnomes were thought to be tiny hunchbacks ruled over by King Gob, who had a magic sword. In German stories their king was called Rübezahl. He was kind to good people but would punish anyone who made fun of him. In Iceland, gnomes are called vættir. No-one in Iceland wants to disturb the vættir, so if a road is likely to run through a place where they live, it will be diverted to leave them in peace.

The Alps, the highest mountains in Europe, are home to a race of gnomes called the barbegazi (from the French *barbe*, meaning beard, and *glacée*, meaning ice). They dress in white fur and have icicles hanging from their long, white beards. The barbegazi have huge feet, which they use as skis or snowshoes, and they like nothing better than surfing atop avalanches and playing in the snow. These caretakers of the mountains are kindly towards humans as long as they treat the environment with respect. They will give a warning hoot if an avalanche is coming and even dig people out of the snow.

GARDEN GNOMES

Pottery gnomes are popular garden ornaments. These comical, brightly-colored figures are usually shown fishing or gardening. The very first garden gnomes were made in Germany over 150 years ago. They were inspired by local legends that said gnomes liked to help in the garden at night and were turned to stone during the day. Garden gnomes soon became popular in Germany, France, and Britain. Today, there are at least 25,000,000 garden gnomes in Germany; that's about one for every family! The oldest garden gnome in Britain is called Lampy and is worth one million pounds.

Left *Kindly gnomes live underground, where they often keep hoards of gold. They are friends to woodland creatures and keen gardeners.*

WONDER WORKERS

Throughout the centuries there have been people who are different from those around them, who have special powers, either inborn or learned, that set them apart. Some have magical abilities, others might be able to speak to the dead or walk in the world of spirits. Some, like certain wizards or the mysterious djinn, are not even human at all. How real are their powers? Enter the world of magic—the domain of witches and wizards, shamans, and spirit walkers—and decide for yourself.

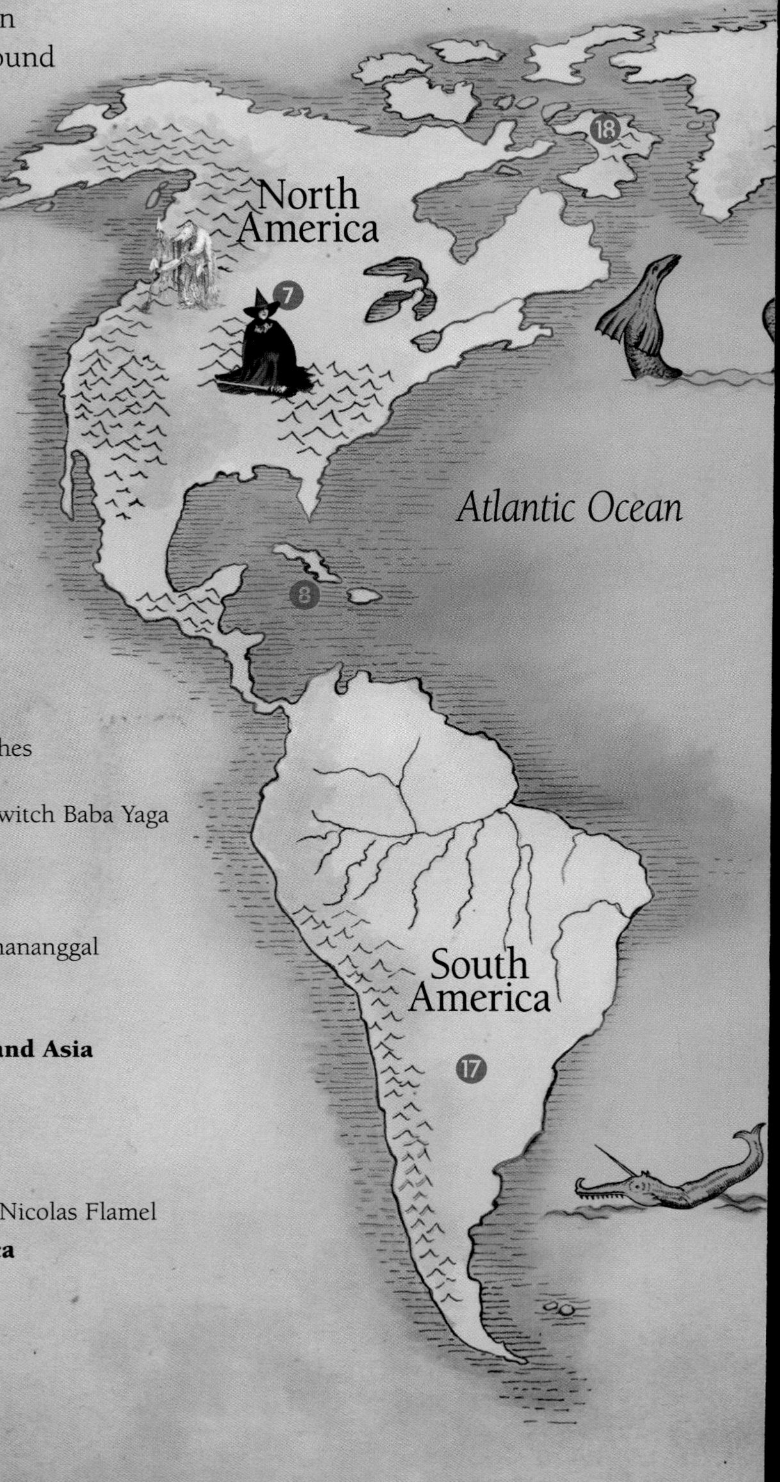

North America

Atlantic Ocean

South America

❶ Middle East
Djinn, witches

❷ Europe
Witches, wizards, spiritualists

❸ Greece
The sorceress Circe

❹ Wales
Merlin, wizard to King Arthur

❺ United Kingdom
Nimue, sorceress lover of Merlin, Witch-finder General Matthew Hopkins, royal astrologer John Dee, witches, wizards, spiritualists

❻ Germany
Dr Faustus, who sold his soul to the devil

❼ North America
Spiritualists Kate and Margaret Fox, witches, wizards, shamans, Salem witches

❽ Caribbean
Voudou witch doctors, shamans

❾ Africa
Shamans, witches

❿ Russia
The terrifying witch Baba Yaga

⓫ India
Witches

⓬ Philippines
The flying manananggal

⓭ China
Mystics

⓮ Middle East and Asia
Jinn demons

⓯ North Africa
Djinn

⓰ France
The alchemist Nicolas Flamel

⓱ South America
Shamans

⓲ Arctic region
Shamans

Arctic Ocean

Europe

Asia

Pacific Ocean

Africa

Indian Ocean

Australia

N
W   E
S

WITCHES AND ENCHANTRESSES

The word "witch" comes from an Old English word meaning to bend or change, and witches are people who can bend or change reality by magical means. Witches take all sorts of forms depending on where in the world they come from, but the one thing they all have in common is their ability to perform magic—sometimes for good but more often for evil.

Above *Hapless Hansel and Gretel, lost in the woods, approach the gingerbread house of a wicked, child-eating witch, in an illustration of the fairy tale by the Brothers Grimm.*

Almost every country has its own stories about witches and witchcraft. In Europe and North America witches are usually ugly old crones who fly on broomsticks and cook up wicked spells in their cauldrons. They might have animal companions called familiars, such as cats, owls, and toads. People in medieval times believed witches' familiars were really demons in disguise. In folk tales, such as Hansel and Gretel, witches often have a taste for eating children! Some stories show witches as beautiful enchantresses, who are born with magical powers and may even be immortal, such as the beautiful Circe of Greek legend.

Witches of the Navajo people of North America are usually men and have the ability to shape-shift by wearing the skin of the animal they wish to become. In African folklore witches look just like ordinary people and might not even realize they have magical powers. India has many tales of witchcraft. In one story, an ugly old witch shape-shifts into a beautiful woman

Fantastical fact
〰〰〰

Men can be witches too. Male witches are sometimes called warlocks.

Right *The traditional image of a witch—in ragged clothes and wearing a pointed hat, riding astride a broomstick—is hundreds of years old.*

and marries a king. After their wedding, he finds his horses, cows, and even elephants are all disappearing. It turns out his greedy witch-wife has been swallowing them whole!

BROOMSTICKS AND CAULDRONS

Some witches, like the manananggal, a sorceress from the Philippines, can fly. The manananggal splits herself in two and her top half flies off to terrorize people. But most witches need something to fly on or in, such as broomsticks. This idea probably started hundreds of years ago because brooms were handy and commonplace. Some witches have even been known to fly on pitchforks and spades! In Russia, the horrifying witch Baba Yaga flies around in a mortar (a vessel for grinding herbs).

The other thing that witches do is cast spells—magic that makes things happen or change. Some witches cast spells with just the power of their minds, a wave of their hand, or a muttered incantation. Others use magical brews containing disgusting ingredients, such as bats' wings, rats' tails, and dragons' blood, often concocted in large, black cauldrons. Just like broomsticks, cauldrons were common household items turned to sinister use by witches.

CIRCE AND ODYSSEUS

In Greek legend, Odysseus was a hero who had many adventures on the long voyage home from a great war. One day, his ship landed at an island where Circe, a beautiful enchantress, lived. Odysseus sent a party of men to explore the island. They came to Circe's palace and she offered them shelter and food. But she drugged their drinks then turned them into wild pigs. Luckily, one man escaped to tell Odysseus what had happened. Odysseus rushed to the palace. On the way he was met by the god Hermes, who gave him a magic plant to protect him against Circe's witchcraft. When Circe's spell did not work on him, she was terrified. He threatened to kill her unless she turned his men back, so she did. In the end Odysseus and his men stayed on the island and Odysseus and Circe had three sons.

Right *Beautiful enchantress Circe was the daughter of Helios the sun god and Hecate, goddess of the moon and witchcraft, from whom she undoubtedly got her magic powers.*

WITCHES ON TRIAL

People have been frightened of witches and witchcraft for hundreds of years. In the middle ages in Europe more than 200,000 people were executed for practicing witchcraft. Amazingly, in some parts of the world witch-hunting still goes on today.

I t was no fun being a child in the Puritan village of Salem, America, in 1692. Puritans were God-fearing Christians who followed very strict religious rules. They thought playing games was wicked and children were expected to be seen and not heard. So when nine-year-old Betty Parris started acting very strangely, throwing fits, making weird noises, and crawling under furniture, the grown-ups took it very seriously. Soon, several other girls began acting the same way. They said they had been bewitched, and they accused three women of witchcraft, including Tituba, a slave in Betty's household. Tituba said a mysterious dark man had made her do wicked things, such as riding in the air on a pole and signing the Devil's book.

Below *The wild accounts of demons and witchcraft given by the young girls of Salem were probably inspired by a servant's voudou tales.*

FLYING ACCUSATIONS

This confession and the girls' continued bizarre behavior and accusations whipped up a witch-hunting frenzy. In the end over 150 people were imprisoned for witchcraft, including a four-year-old girl and an 80-year-old man. Nineteen people were hanged, and then the girls began accusing people in other villages, too. They finally went a step too far when they pointed the finger at the wife of the Governor, the man in charge. He had the trials stopped and released everyone. The nightmare was over as suddenly as it had begun.

But why did the girls do it? Some think they were influenced by stories of voudou told to them by Tituba, others that it was simple rebellion that spiralled out of control. We'll probably never know the complete story.

Above *Hundreds of years ago witches were believed to practice black magic, to be able to fly, to worship the Devil at wild gatherings called sabbats, and to have evil spirits, called familiars, as companions.*

How to identify a witch

When witch-hunting in Europe was at its height, all of these were thought to be signs of being a witch. As you can see, few people were safe!

- Having a mole or mark on the body
- Owning a black cat
- Talking to yourself
- Talking to animals
- Spinning around
- Having red hair or freckles
- Having unusual eyes

WITCH-FINDER GENERAL

In 1647, a man called Matthew Hopkins decided it was his duty to find and destroy all witches in England. At that time the country was in the middle of a civil war, and Hopkins took advantage of everyone's fear and mistrust. He styled himself "Witch-finder General" and went from village to village getting people to accuse their neighbors of witchcraft. Anyone remotely unpopular or suspicious could find themselves put on trial. Hopkins tested them for witchcraft, tortured them, and examined their bodies for birthmarks or blemishes, which he said were marks of the Devil. He ordered the deaths of over 230 people, charging handsomely for his services. But this was his undoing—people got tired of paying him, and the trials stopped.

Above *Witch-finder General Matthew Hopkins examines a witch and her familiars.*

WIZARDS AND MAGICIANS

Wizards and magicians are people with mysterious and magical powers. Some learn their magical skills, while others are born with special abilities. And not all wizards are men—some are women, and some wizards are not human at all.

Wizard means wise, and wizards are often thought of as wise old men with long, white beards who have spent a lifetime acquiring great knowledge and skills in magic. But originally a wizard was any wise man or woman. Hundreds of years ago, almost every village in Europe had its own wizard. At that time people believed that their misfortunes, such as failed harvests, accidents, and illnesses, were caused by curses, demons, or simply by someone wishing them bad luck. It was the wizard's job to sort these things out by casting out demons and removing curses. They would also do fortune telling, divining (finding things), healing, and spell-casting.

In India and China, wizards were more concerned with honing their own powers than helping others. Indian fakirs, for example, tended to spend their time away from other people developing skills such as snake charming and levitation. Some Chinese mystics practised wushu—martial arts—with such total dedication that their abilities became magical, allowing them to fly through the air and use weapons with total accuracy.

Fantastical fact

Magicians and conjurers today, who do magic tricks for entertainment, don't claim to use real magic. Their tricks are illusions, using sleight of hand (stealthy movements that deceive the eye) and other clever techniques.

Above In the German story of Dr Faustus the main character sold his soul to the devil in return for 24 years' worth of knowledge and magical power. He lived to regret it—when his time was up a host of demons came and dragged his soul to hell!

REAL-LIFE WIZARDS

There have always been real people who have practiced magic and wizardry in various forms. Dr John Dee (1527–1608), for instance, was like a cross between a magician and a scientist. In his time people explained lots of things that we understand scientifically today by the power of magic. Dee was a mathematician, alchemist (see box below), an astrologer, and he became an adviser to Queen Elizabeth I of England on such matters. Dr Dee was accused of witchcraft but was saved from persecution because of his royal connections.

Nicolas Flamel was an alchemist. He was born in France in 1330 and was supposed to have discovered the secret of immortality. The story goes that when his coffin was opened by grave robbers there was no body—because he was immortal, Flamel had faked his own death and carried on living in his home city of Paris in secret.

ALCHEMY

Alchemists believed in the existence of a "philosopher's stone," a magical substance that could turn ordinary metal into gold, cure disease, and make you live forever. Today, science tells us that such things are probably impossible, but hundreds of years ago alchemists truly believed they could find the answers to these secrets through spells and experiments. In many ways alchemists were the forerunners of today's scientists. They came up with theories and carried out experiments to try and prove their ideas. Alchemy can be traced back to ancient Egypt. It was also practiced in China, India, and Arabia. In Europe many alchemists were persecuted as wizards.

Above Alchemists worked in laboratories.

FAMOUS WIZARDS

Wizards have appeared in myths, fairy tales, and modern stories for centuries in roles ranging from hero to villain. They also often play parts as teachers or guardians. Merlin is probably one of the most famous wizards in the world. He is well known as the wise magician who served the legendary King Arthur of England in the court of Camelot, but there are many other tales in which he is very different, even terrifying! The story that follows is just one version of his life.

MERLIN AND KING ARTHUR

Merlin was the son of a nun and a demon. The moment he was born his mother plunged him into holy water to try and rid him of any evil he may have inherited from his father. When he grew up, Merlin became the friend and helper of the English king, Uther Pendragon. Uther fell in love with Ygraine, the wife of the duke of Cornwall, but she would have nothing to do with him. Uther asked Merlin to use his magic to enable him to spend a night with her. So Merlin enchanted Uther to make him look like the duke and took him to Ygraine. She was fooled by the disguise and a child, Arthur, was born of their union that night.

Merlin knew it was Arthur's destiny to unite the country, which was divided by war. To keep him safe, Merlin took Arthur when he was born and gave him to a foster family, so neither his family nor Arthur himself knew who he really was. Merlin was able to watch over him as he grew up. Arthur's destiny was finally revealed when he pulled a magical sword from where it was embedded in a stone—something only the future king could do. Once Arthur was king, Merlin helped him bring together a band of brave and good knights, the Knights of the Round Table. Under Arthur's leadership, they brought peace to the country for many years. Merlin was Arthur's guide and helper throughout his life, but even he could not

Left *The sorceress Nimue enchants Merlin, sending him into a deep sleep so she can read from his book of spells.*

prevent Arthur's eventual death—he was killed by his own son, Mordred, who wanted to be king in his place. Merlin did foretell, however, that Arthur will be healed and come to Britain's aid once again.

Merlin's own death came at the hands of an enchantress called Nimue, or Viviane. Nimue fell in love with Merlin, but he believed her to be evil and rejected her. She finally tricked him by turning herself into a lovely young maiden. Merlin was enchanted by her beauty, but when he embraced her, she turned them both into an oak tree. They remain there, entwined, to this very day.

Right *Gandalf the Grey is the good wizard in J.R.R. Tolkein's stories of Middle Earth,* The Hobbit *and* The Lord of the Rings. *Gandalf guides the other characters in their quest to destroy a powerful ring and save Middle Earth from the evil Sauron.*

HARRY POTTER

In the immensely popular Harry Potter books by J.K. Rowling, there exists a parallel "wizarding world" where witches and wizards go about their daily lives hidden from the normal, or "muggle" world. Harry is the hero of the books, which recount his life growing up at Hogwart's School of Wizardry and Witchcraft. Here he makes friends and enemies, learns his craft, and fights the forces of evil—in particular the devilish Voldemort, a terrifying wizard who killed Harry's parents when Harry was a baby. The books are full of weird and wonderful characters, scary monsters, and thrilling adventures. Like any good hero, Harry has to go through many trials in which his special powers are tested to the very limit. Does he succeed in defeating Voldemort? You'll have to read the books to find out!

Above *Boy wizard Harry Potter casts powerful spells.*

DJINN

Djinn, often called genies, are magical beings, both dangerous and powerful, born of fire. They have the ability to grant wishes, but they can also trick the wisher and turn their desires against them, so be careful what you wish for.

There are several tales about djinn, including "Aladdin," "The Fisherman and the Djnni," and "Sindbad the Sailor," in a famous collection of Arabian stories called *The Book of One Thousand and One Nights* or *Arabian Nights* (see page 39). In "Aladdin" there are two djinn, one trapped in a ring and a second, more powerful djinni, inside an old lamp. They are released when someone rubs the ring or the lamp and grant wishes in return. In the other two stories, Sindbad and the fisherman release angry djinn from sealed jars. Djinn have the power to grant wishes, but usually only three. When people use their wishes unwisely, it can have disastrous effects, and djinn sometimes willfully misunderstand wishes, causing more harm than good.

Stories about djinn and genies were probably inspired by the Qur'an—the holy book of the religion of Islam—which tells of a race of beings called the Jinn. These Jinn are a bit like humans but stronger and not so clever. They eat, marry, and die just like humans but live much longer. The Jinn were made by Allah from smokeless fire and are usually invisible. They live in remote forests and mountains. Some Jinn harass people, but most don't bother humans.

This page *Traditionally, magical djinn were often imprisoned in small objects, such as bottles and lamps, and released when the stopper was removed.*

Fantastical fact

In Moroccan folklore the Maezt Dar l'Oudou is a monstrous, goat-shaped djinni that haunts toilets!

THE FISHERMAN AND THE DJINNI

A fisherman cast his net into the sea and pulled out a strange brass vessel. When he removed the stopper, a huge plume of smoke came rushing out and took the form of a giant djinni. The djinni said he had been trapped in the vessel for hundreds of years. When he was first imprisoned, he told the fisherman, he had promised himself he would grant anyone who released him any wishes they wanted, but as the years passed the djinni got angrier and angrier and more and more ruthless, until in the end he decided he would kill anyone who released him, only giving them a choice about the way they would die. Terrified, the fisherman kept the djinni talking while he tried to think of a way to avoid being killed. Finally, he came up with a brilliant idea. The djinni was vain and full of his own importance, so the fisherman started to express doubts that such a huge and powerful being as himself could possibly have fitted into such a small vessel. Infuriated that the fisherman didn't believe him, the djinni disappeared back into the vessel to prove it. In a flash, the fisherman picked up the stopper and firmly sealed the brass vessel again with the djinni inside.

SCHEHERAZADE'S ARABIAN NIGHTS

There once was a great king whose wife was unfaithful to him. He was so enraged that he had her executed and then began marrying a succession of new wives only to execute them the morning after the wedding. Eventually he decided to marry Scheherazade, the daughter of his chief minister. Scheherazade was cleverer than her predecessors. On their wedding night she began to tell the king a story, but when she got to a particularly exciting part, she stopped. The king was so curious to hear the end of the story that he put off the execution so that she could tell it to him the next day. The next night, she finished the tale and immediately started a new one, again stopping half way through. The king had to delay her execution once more.

This went on night after night as Scheherazade related fairy tales, comedies, tragedies, and poems featuring heroes, djinn, princesses, and monsters. In this way she managed to stay her execution for 1001 nights, until the king died.

Left *Clever Scheherazade kept her murderous husband guessing with her exciting stories for more than three years, thus ensuring her survival.*

SPIRITUALISTS

How would you like to speak to the dead? Many people have claimed to be able to see, hear, and communicate with the spirits of those who have died. They call themselves spiritualists or mediums, but do they really have a hotline to the grave?

A hundred and fifty years ago there were no such things as televisions, movies, computers, or even radios, so people had to find other entertainments. Séances—meetings where people attempted to communicate with the dead—became a popular pastime in both Europe and America.

SUPERNATURAL VISITORS?

At a séance everyone would sit around a table and link hands or touch fingers to form a circle. The leader of the séance, called a medium, would ask everyone to concentrate hard while he or she tried to make contact with the dead. Mediums might use what they called their spirit guide, a friendly spirit who would lead them to other dead souls. Often the people attending would hope to communicate with someone they knew who had died.

All sorts of weird things might happen at a séance—the table might move, objects might appear or levitate (rise into the air), the medium might convey messages through strange "automatic" writing, and there might be unexplained knocking sounds or other noises. Some witnesses claimed to see shadows of the spirits themselves or a ghostly white substance called ectoplasm oozing from people's heads.

Many people were convinced that these events were real, but others were certain it was all trickery. Some but not all of the mediums were exposed as frauds. Clever devices or hidden accomplices were often used to move furniture, make noises, or pose as spirits, and "ectoplasm" usually turned out to be egg white, chewed up paper, or fine muslin. There were even people sent to prison for faking supernatural events at séances.

Above The use of muslin cloth to represent ectoplasm was a trick used by spiritualist fraudsters— not a very convincing one!

Right *At a Victorian séance you might expect strange voices, noises, moving objects, and even the appearance of a spirit.*

THE FOX SISTERS

The craze for spiritualism was sparked off in the U.S.A. in 1848 when two sisters, Kate and Margaret Fox, reported hearing strange rapping sounds in their home in New York. The girls developed a form of communication, in which a certain number of raps might indicate "yes" or "no" or signify a letter of the alphabet. They said the noises were coming from the spirit of a murdered peddler whose body was buried in the cellar. Kate and Margaret began holding séances where all sorts of supernatural events occurred and their fame grew. A new movement called spiritualism grew up around them and attending séances became very fashionable. Later the sisters confessed that they had faked the rapping sounds by secretly cracking their joints! But as for the murdered pedlar— almost fifty years later, in 1904, a skeleton with a peddler's tin was found bricked up inside the Foxes' cellar wall!

POLTERGEISTS

Poltergeists are restless, sometimes violent spirits that move objects. They will sometimes focus on one particular person, most often a teenage girl. Poltergeist is German for "knocking ghost," and poltergeist hauntings often involve knocking or other strange noises as well as the moving or throwing of objects. Poltergeist activity has never been satisfactorily explained. Some instances have been shown to be hoaxes. Others are thought to be caused by people using psychokinesis (movement of objects with the power of the mind).

Left *Is the mysterious movement of objects, apparently of their own accord, caused by poltergeists, telekinesis, or trickery?*

SHAMANS

Enter the world of the shamans—people who can communicate with spirits. Shamans can use their special abilities for good or for evil: to cast spells, heal the sick, see into the future, predict or control the weather, and seek answers to burning questions.

Shamans are important people in many human communities, especially those that live closely with nature, such as the Inuit of the Arctic and tribes of the Amazon rainforest. They share a belief that all things in nature have a spirit, and that these spirits can affect human lives and actions. For example, when people need to hunt animals for food, shamans might speak with the spirits of the animals, asking permission to hunt them. If the animal spirits are properly respected, they will willingly allow themselves to be killed.

Shamans are very mystical and might communicate with the spirits through music, dances, drawings, or symbols. In order to enter the spirit world and gain knowledge or seek answers to questions, such as how to heal someone who is sick, they will sometimes need to leave their body. To do this, the shaman will normally go into a trance, allowing their own spirit to fly free of their body.

GIFT OR CURSE?

Not just anyone can become a shaman. You either have to be the child of a shaman and inherit their powers or be especially chosen by the spirits. Often, people are chosen in their youth during a serious illness. In the course of the illness they are visited by spirits and given special knowledge. The

Right *This Inuit mask was carved for a shaman to wear. It shows how the shaman could see inside the body to cure sickness. The Inuit people live in the Arctic regions of North America.*

training for a shaman, when they learn to visit the spirits and understand what the spirits tell them, can be long and arduous. They may experience terrifying visions as they undergo the transformation. Most shamans are men, but female shamans do exist.

Shamans usually work for the good of their people, but even so, their great knowledge and power sets them apart from ordinary men and women, and they are often feared or kept at a distance.

Left *A shaman from a Siberian tribe uses bells on his costume and a hand drum to make music during a ceremonial dance.*

Fantastical fact

Shamanism is one of the oldest human beliefs. It can be traced back at least 20,000 years!

NATURE WORSHIPERS

Not just people living closely with nature have a strong connection with the natural and spirit worlds. Followers of a religion called Wicca in Europe, North America, and elsewhere are worshipers of nature in the form of a God and Goddess. Wiccans sometimes also call themselves witches, but this modern witchcraft is very different from the black magic feared in medieval times. Wiccans do not practice any black arts (sorcery used for dark, harmful purposes) but strongly believe in the hidden powers of the mind to do good. There are more Wiccan witches active in the world today than ever before in history—probably 130,000 in the U.S.A. alone.

Right *A follower of Wicca is performing a ritual here. Spell casting and rituals are an important part of Wiccan practice.*

Evil Spirits, Demons, and the Undead

S hambling mummies brought back to life after thousands of years; terrifying rotting corpses leaving their graves and walking among the living—this is the stuff of nightmares and Hollywood movies. Humans have an endless fascination with the cheating of death by whatever method: using magic and spells, drinking blood, or returning in ghostly form. Then there are the creatures that personify evil—demons, werewolves, and evil spirits. Stories of such beings are common in all cultures. So, are they real or just the product of universal human fears?

Atlantic Ocean

North America

South America

Worldwide
Demons, ghosts

1 Egypt
Mummies

2 Caribbean
Zombies

3 Africa
Zombies, vampires

4 India
The bloodthirsty goddess Kali

5 Israel
The vampire demon Lilith, golems

6 Japan
Vampires, kitsunebi, treacherous fox spirits

7 Eastern Europe
Vampires, including Dracula

8 Europe
Demons, ghosts, vampires, evil spirits

9 Romania
Dracula, Vlad the Impaler

10 Ireland
Banshees, the Dullahan

11 England
Will-o'-the-wisps, vampires, werewolves

12 Scotland
The doom-bringing washer woman

13 U.S.A.
Vampires, jack-o'-lanterns

14 South America
Vampires

Arctic Ocean

Europe

Africa

Asia

Indian Ocean

Pacific Ocean

Australia

VAMPIRES

Vampires are characters straight out of our most horrifying dreams. They are the "undead"—unfortunate victims of vampire attacks who have died but refuse to lie down—rising from their graves at night to drink the blood of the living and keep themselves "alive." Vampires can turn their victims into monsters like themselves, doomed to stalk the dark shadows for eternity.

Stories of blood-drinking monsters are nothing new. Ancient Egyptians told tales of Sekhmet, a blood-gorging goddess, and the ancient Indian goddess Kali was another terrifying bloodsucker, complete with fangs. Hebrew tradition tells of Lilith, a revolting demon who lived in the blood of babies. There are bloodsucking characters in Greek and Roman myths; and China, Japan, India, Canada, and Africa all have their own tales of vampire monsters. But the bloodthirsty vampires we usually think of today are night-walking, pale, gaunt figures with fang-like teeth that they use to bite the necks of their prey. These fiends were invented in the 19th century by writers of horror stories, who were themselves inspired by folk tales from Eastern Europe.

Above *Bram Stoker's book has inspired generations of vampire stories.*

COUNT DRACULA

Count Dracula, the most famous vampire of all, made his first appearance in a book written over 100 years ago, yet he still has the power to fascinate us. The book tells the story of an evil count who travels to England from his native Transylvania and terrorizes two young women and their friends. Dracula makes a vampire of one girl and almost kills the other before being hunted down and destroyed by the vampire hunter Professor van Helsing and his team.

Bram Stoker, the Irish author of Dracula, apparently based the Count's appearance on his friend Henry Irving, a famous actor. The book wasn't particularly popular at first, and it wasn't until Dracula films started to be made in the 20th century that it became a classic. The novel has inspired more than 60 films, and today vampires still provide popular material for books, films, television series, and computer games.

REAL-LIFE DRACULA

Bram Stoker probably got the name "Dracula" from Vlad III, a prince of Wallachia (in present day Romania) almost 600 years ago. His surname was Dracula or "son of Dracul" (*dracul* meant dragon in Romanian at the time), and he was a very nasty piece of work. Vlad had an original way of dealing with anyone who annoyed him; he would impale them on a pointed stake, leaving them to die in agony. He carried out these punishments on a vast scale, sometimes by the hundreds or thousands. He even had the stakes arranged in patterns and was said to have once held a dinner party in the middle of a forest of impaled victims.

Left Max Schreck cut a terrifying figure as a vampire in the 1922 film Nosferatu.

Above Was this the original Dracula? Vlad the Impaler was a medieval mass murderer.

Right U.S. television series Buffy the Vampire Slayer *explored the inner psyche of the vampire. Its characters were locked in a constant struggle between good and evil.*

MUMMIES

An ancient tomb is opened. The mummy inside is awoken from its long sleep of death and wreaks a terrible revenge on those who dared to disturb it. It makes a great story, doesn't it? But the idea that Egyptian mummies can come back to life was invented by Hollywood film-makers.

A mummy is any dead body that is preserved instead of rotting away. Mummification can happen naturally—for instance if a corpse is buried in very dry conditions—or artificially, with the use of various drying or embalming techniques. The ancient Egyptians believed that after death the soul, or ka, of the dead person travelled to the afterlife, where it would live happily, much as it had done in life. Rich or important people in particular were mummified and buried with all the possessions they might need. Mummification wasn't only done in ancient Egypt; artificially preserved mummies have also been found in South America and Europe.

THE MUMMY'S CURSE

One of the most famous Egyptian mummies was that of the boy pharaoh Tutankhamun, discovered in 1922 by Howard Carter and Lord Carnarvon. Despite huge public interest, Carter refused to release any details to the newspapers, so they started making things up. One rumor was about a curse promising death to those who entered the pharaoh's tomb. When Lord Carnarvon died just six weeks later, closely followed by two other people linked to the dig, the curse story took off. But Howard Carter, the first person to enter the tomb, strongly dismissed the idea and died of natural causes 17 years later.

Above Howard Carter (kneeling) takes a first glimpse into Tutankhamun's tomb.

Left The preservation of this unidentified mummy found near Cairo is so good that its features are still clearly defined.

Right In the 1950s and 60s Hammer, the famous horror-movie studio, made several films featuring a bandaged mummy as a shambling, murderous monster. More recently The Mummy (1999) and its sequels have used computer-generated effects to create the most terrifying mummy yet.

How to make an ancient Egyptian mummy

- First of all wash and dry the body. You need to work quickly before it starts to decompose.

- The body won't need that gray, slushy brain—it serves no purpose. Shove a special hook up the corpse's nose and into the skull. Whisk it around to liquefy the brain, so you can pull or pour it out. Fill the skull with resin.

- You need to take out the lungs, liver, stomach, and intestines. Cut the body open and remove these—cover them with natron (a drying salt) for 40 days. Leave the heart, as this is the organ used for thinking and the body will need it in the afterlife. Wash the body cavity out with wine and add some natron. Leave for 40 days.

- Check your removed organs. When they are completely dried out, put them into special canopic jars to be stored with the body.

- After 40 days in natron your body should also be ready. The skin will be shriveled up and wrinkled, so it will need to be rubbed with perfumed oils to soften it up a bit.

- Fill the body cavity with anything you have to hand—sawdust or old rags is fine.

- You should then make the finishing touches, such as replacing the eyeballs (which will have shriveled away in the natron). Small onions are good for this. You can fill any cracks or hollows in the skin with mud.

- Put protectors over the fingers and toes to stop them getting broken.

- Now you are ready for the wrapping. You will need lots of linen strips. Start with the head and work down, sealing the wrappings with resin as you go. You will need about 20 layers and the entire process might take up to 2 weeks. Place a few lucky charms, called amulets, between the bandages as you wrap. These will protect the mummy from harm.

- Finally, wrap your mummy in one large canvas sheet and bind firmly.

- Your mummy is ready to be put into its coffin!

ZOMBIES AND GOLEMS

The living dead—zombies—are amongst the most terrifying of monsters. Because they are already dead, you can't kill them. Both zombies and golems—mindless creatures made from clay—are controlled by magical forces and are strangers to reason.

Fantastical fact

A mixture of chemicals from the highly venomous puffer fish and the skin of a poisonous toad can make a person's breath so shallow and their heartbeat so weak that they will appear to be dead. The poison doesn't even have to be swallowed; it's enough to just rub it on the skin.

On the island of Hispaniola in the Carribean sea 400 years ago, African slaves were taken to Haiti to work on sugar plantations. They took their African spiritual beliefs with them but were forced by their owners to convert to Catholic Christianity. Voudou, or Voodoo, is a complicated mixture of these two religions. According to one of their beliefs, Vodou sorcerers could bring the dead back to life and turn them into zombies—slaves that would do whatever the sorcerer told them. "Zombie" comes from an African word that means spirit of a dead person. Although raising the dead sounds far-fetched, there have been incredible stories from people who claim to have been turned into zombies.

MAN OF CLAY

Similar to a zombie is the Jewish monster called a golem. It was said that powerful

FRANKENSTEIN'S MONSTER

Perhaps the most famous creature to be raised from the dead is Frankenstein's monster. It's hard to believe, but the classic horror story was written almost 200 years ago and by an 18-year-old girl! The writer was Mary Shelley, who married the famous poet Percy Bysshe Shelley, while she was writing the book.

Her story tells of the ambitious scientist Victor Frankenstein, who believes he can create life. He makes a huge man from pieces of dead bodies and uses electricity to bring his creation to life. The unfortunate creature is hideous. He is cast out by the scientist and unwittingly terrorizes almost everyone who crosses his path. Eventually, out of anger, he murders people close to Frankenstein and flees to the Arctic. Frankenstein follows him, but dies before he can find him. When the monster learns of his creator's death, he is filled with sorrow. The book ends with him walking away across the Arctic ice, never to be seen again.

Above Victor Frankenstein recoiled with horror when his creation came to life.

rabbis (Jewish teachers) could create human-shaped creatures from clay and use spells to turn them into slaves. Golems couldn't speak and had no will of their own. If a rabbi's power over a golem were somehow lost, the mindless creature would simply turn to dust.

Above *According to Jewish legend, the way to bring a golem to life is to write a holy word on its forehead.*

Right *The classic film image of Frankenstein's monster was perfected by the English actor Boris Karloff.*

THE STRANGE CASE OF CLAIRVIUS NARCISSE

In May 1962 a Haitian man called Clairvius Narcisse died in hospital after a short illness. He was buried the next day. Eighteen years later, his sister bumped into him in a market—alive and well! He told her an incredible story. Back in 1962, he and his brother had quarreled violently. The brother had then paid someone, a slave master and Voudou sorcerer, to poison him. The poison made it look as though Clairvius was dead. Shortly after his burial he was dug up, revived, and given more drugs that brainwashed him.

He was sent to a sugar plantation where he worked for two years alongside other zombie slaves. When the slave master died, Clairvius managed to escape, and he drifted through life for the next 16 years gradually recovering and terrified that he might come across his brother again. Luckily, by the time he found his sister, the brother had died. Later investigations revealed that his grave had indeed been opened and that Voudou drugs could cause the effects Clairvius experienced. So was his story true? No one really knows.

GHOSTS

Have you ever seen a ghost? Spirits of the dead are the most widely reported supernatural phenomena in the world and ghost stories are common to most cultures. In many countries ghosts are taken very seriously. In China, for example, the hungry ghost festival is held to prevent restless spirits from harming people. But what are ghosts, and do they really exist?

Fantastical fact

Ghostly apparitions are not always human in form. There have been reports of ghost trains and ships that appear out of nowhere—constantly replaying their final voyage or journey.

Experts on the paranormal suggest that there are two types of ghosts or hauntings. The first is a bit like a recording—an event from the past that is somehow stored in the area or building where it happened and "replays" when the conditions are right. This is a bit like watching a film or D.V.D. playback—it is the same every time and you can't interact with it or change what is going on. The recorded event is often something dramatic, such as a sudden death or a murder.

The second type of haunting involves the earthbound spirit of a dead person. The ghost might take the form of the person who has died, or it might manifest itself as some form of energy, such as sounds, lights, touches, or moving objects. Some hauntings cause a drop in temperature or a distinctive smell, such as perfume or cigarette smoke. Unlike the first type, these phenomena can and do interact with people. This can be scary for the people involved, but ghost watchers think that most of the time ghosts are relatively harmless. Experts think that spirits of the dead can be earthbound for many different reasons: they may be seeking revenge for a violent death; or they may have unfinished business they feel compelled to complete, such as a message to give to someone. Such ghosts are usually tied to a particular place.

ARE GHOSTS EVIL?

A ghost might be good or bad the same way a person might be good or bad in life. Some ghosts may be mischievous pranksters and others may be trying to control their surroundings. Perhaps they want humans to leave them alone or to leave the place that they haunt. There are sometimes reports of malevolent hauntings, but many experts on the paranormal believe these to be caused by evil spirits, such as demons, rather than human ghosts.

Right *The traditional image of a ghost is of a silent, transparent specter floating just above the ground.*

Below *Some say spectral vessels like this ghostly galleon are doomed to continually repeat their final voyage.*

ARE GHOSTS REAL?

Belief in ghosts, including the conjuring up of spirits and exorcism (getting rid of them), has also been part of many religions for centuries. However, there is no real proof that ghosts actually exist. Most evidence is in the form of eye-witness reports. There is little doubt that many people truly believe that they have seen ghosts. Have they mistaken something perfectly ordinary for a ghostly occurrence, or have they been the victims of a hoax or even of their own imaginations? In the last 150 years, ghosts have been the subject of more scientific investigation. Parapsychologists have tried to categorize ghostly phenomena and give them specific names and definitions, but many photographs and recordings of so-called ghost activity are eventually exposed as frauds or explained by something quite ordinary, such as electrical disturbances or the fogging of camera film.

Right *The figure in this photograph was dubbed "the Brown Lady of Raynham Hall." The image, taken in 1936, is not thought to have been faked or tampered with in any way. Could it be genuine evidence of a ghost?*

DEATHLY SPIRITS

Mysterious lights, blood-curdling screams, gory specters, and headless horsemen—beware all these omens, as they can mean only one thing … death! And there is no escape. Deathly spirits such as these are known all over the world.

Above *This mischievous will-o'-the-wisp is using his flickering light to lead unwary travelers into a dangerous bog.*

Flickering, ghostly lights that dance across the ground go by many names: will-o'-the-wisps, hinkypunk, jack-o'-lanterns, corpse lights, hobby lanterns, and corpse candles; and they all spell trouble. They can lure people into danger or death in treacherous bogs and marshlands or foretell death. If a corpse light hovers above a house, it means someone is going to die. If it glows red, the doomed person is male, if white, a female. Across Europe will-o'-the-wisps are thought to be mischievous spirits of the dead who lead travelers into danger, but some can mark the position of treasure—if anyone dares to go and look, that is.

One tale, from Shropshire in England, tells of Will the wicked blacksmith who led such a bad life that he was doomed by Saint Peter to wander the Earth forever. The Devil, feeling sorry for one of his own, gave Will a brightly burning coal to keep warm. Wicked Will uses this devilish light to this day to lead people into the marshes, where they get horribly lost. In Japan, such lights are called kitsunebi or foxfire. Kitsune are trickster foxes who use the lights to mislead unwary travelers.

BANSHEES AND THE WASHER WOMAN

A famous Irish omen of death is the banshee. These female spirits are heard more often than they are seen, but they are usually described as being dressed in white or grey

Do's and don'ts

- **Don't** wander about the countryside alone after dark.

- **Don't** follow any mysterious lights that you see, even if you are curious.

- **Don't** look out of your window at night, no matter what you might hear.

- **Don't** look directly at the Dullahan.

- **Do** keep a gold coin handy; it's the one thing that might distract the Dullahan.

with long fair hair that they brush with a silver comb. The terrible wail of a banshee around a house means someone inside is about to die. Some Irish families have their own banshees who will wail for a death in their clan even if that person is far away. Similar to the banshee is the Bean Nighe or Washer at the Ford. This gruesome apparition is seen washing bloodstained linen in rivers and streams. If someone sees their own linen being washed, they will die. The washer woman often appears to soldiers about to die in battle.

Above *The gruesome Washer at the Ford rinses bloodstained linen belonging to those about to die.*

THE DULLAHAN

The Dullahan is the most terrifying of spirit creatures. He is seen after sunset; a headless rider in flowing, dark robes on a magnificent, black stallion galloping wildly across the countryside. For a whip he has a human spine. When he stops he will call someone's name, drawing out their soul. There is no defence. If your name is called, you are doomed. The Dullahan carries his head in his hands and will lift it up high so he can see great distances. Anyone unfortunate enough to see the Dullahan should beware—he will fling blood in their face, which can strike them blind. Sometimes the Dullahan drives a black coach with six horses—they gallop so fast they set the hedgerows alight.

Below *Headless horsemen feature in many ghost stories, such as "The Legend of Sleepy Hollow," in which the main character disappears after encountering such an apparition.*

DEMONS

What could be more terrifying that being taken over by an evil spirit and losing control over everything you do and say? Tales of demonic possession exist all over the world, particularly in Europe. Demons have also been blamed for nightmares, bizarre behavior, illness, and even death.

To the Greeks and Romans, demons were just spirits that were neither good nor evil. In Hebrew Bible stories, demons were spirits of the underworld that could enter the body and give rise to diseases, especially illnesses such as epilepsy, which causes fits or seizures. The only way to get rid of these demons was to draw them out with religious chants in a process called exorcism. In Christian belief, demons are angels who angered God and were cast into hell. Satan, the Devil, is their leader. In Islam demons are evil Jinn who disobeyed Allah. Hindu demons are terrifying supernatural beings, some are the spirits of dead people who led a very wicked life.

DEMONS IN EUROPE

The idea of demons and possession really took hold in Europe in medieval times. The Christian church reckoned there were over seven and half million demons. They named some of the more powerful ones, such as Asmodeus, Astaroth, Baal, Beelzebub, Belial, and Lucifer. Witches

Right *Demons were thought to sit on the chests of sleepers and cause nightmares.*

How to spot a possession

People were thought to be possessed if they:

- ❀ Lived a wicked life
- ❀ Claimed to be possessed
- ❀ Talked to themselves or heard voices
- ❀ Pulled strange or ugly faces
- ❀ Made odd noises
- ❀ Smelled bad
- ❀ Lost weight rapidly
- ❀ Had a distended stomach
- ❀ Vomited excessively
- ❀ Were violent
- ❀ Had fits or seizures
- ❀ Talked about suicide

Nowadays we would explain many of these as symptoms of disease, such as cancer, epilepsy, or mental illness.

Above *This terrifying image of an ugly, black, horned demon comes from a 1957 horror film called* Night of the Demon.

and wizards of the time used grimoires, books of magic, which told them how to conjure demons to do their bidding. Demons were usually portrayed as ugly, black figures with horns, hoofed feet, long tongues, forked tails, and red eyes. They often had wings, too, and could shape-shift into the form of animals such as toads, dogs, and cats. In this form, they might accompany witches as their familiars.

POSSESSION!

In 1631 the peace of the nunnery at Loudon, a small town in France, was shattered by a scandal of demonic possession. A local priest, the devilishly handsome Father Urbaine Grandier, was not as holy as he should be—he had affairs with local women and made enemies of important church officials. One of these enemies hatched a plan to get rid of him. He asked the mother superior of the local convent to pretend that Father Urbaine had possessed her and some of the other nuns. This she did, and the nuns started to have strange fits and seizures.

So far so good, but after a while, the nuns seemed to really believe in their possession by Urbaine and various demons, and their behavior became even more bizarre. All attempts at exorcism, even by Grandier himself, failed. His enemies continued to stack up evidence against him. They had him jailed and finally burned at the stake. The nuns' antics had proved so entertaining that even after Urbaine's death they continued their strange behavior as a sort of medieval tourist attraction!

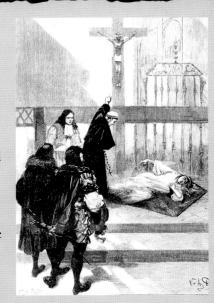

Above *Priests attempted to exorcize demons from the possessed Loudon nuns.*

HUMANOID CREATURES

Many of the creatures that have scared us for generations in myths, legends, and folklore are all the more terrifying for being almost human. There are the hideous female monsters of Greek legend, such as the gorgons and harpies, as well as giants, ogres, and trolls—obscene parodies of humans in their vast proportions and wicked ways. Mysterious and unexplained god-like figures, such as the Green Man, pop up in legends across the world. Stories of men who can turn into ravening beasts are also found worldwide, such as the werewolves of Europe and North America and the Macan Gadungan, the were-tiger of Indonesia.

North America

Atlantic O

South America

❶ Himalayas
The yeti or abominable snowman

❷ North America
Sasquatch or bigfoot, Dzoavits, the Wendigo, the Bokwus, werewolves, skinwalkers

❸ India
Nee-gued, the Green Man

❹ Thailand
The Green Man

❺ Ghana
Tano Giant

❻ South America
Curinquean, werewolves

❼ Indonesia
Macan Gadungan, were-dog

❽ Scandinavia
Trolls

❾ Greece
Cyclopes the one-eyed giants, gorgons, harpies, furies

❿ Europe
Giants, the Green Man, ogres, werewolves

⓫ United Kingdom
Giants, the Green Man, ogres, Herne the Hunter

⓬ Japan
Oni—demon ogres

⓭ Africa
Giants, ogres

⓮ Canada
Trolls

Arctic Ocean

Europe

Asia

Africa

Pacific Ocean

Indian Ocean

Australia

N
W   E
S

WEREWOLVES

It's the dead of night, but a huge, bright full moon casts an unearthly glow over the land. The silence is shattered by a bloodcurdling howl—just the call of a wolf, or is it something much, much more sinister?

WORLD WEREWOLVES

According to legend, a werewolf is a person who turns into a wolf with every full moon and goes on a rampage of death—slaughtering victims, both animal and human, by hunting them down and tearing them to pieces. Although the werewolf returns to its normal human form at daybreak, there is no cure, and the curse will return at the next full moon. The only release is to kill the creature with a silver weapon, such as a knife, arrow, or bullet. You can become a werewolf through being cursed or being bitten by another werewolf.

Werewolf means man-wolf, but wolves are not the only animals that shape-shifters might turn into. In different parts of the world there are legends about were-tigers, -bears, -leopards, -hyenas, and even -crocodiles. The Macan Gadungan, for instance, is a were-tiger from Indonesia. Macan gadungans change themselves intentionally by magic and go on terrifying killing frenzies. The were-dog of the island of Timor has the power to turn people into animals while they sleep. He then eats them!

Above *People who believe they turn into werewolves are called "lycanthropes." The process of transforming into a slavering monster like this is imagined to be both terrifying and intensely painful.*

WEREWOLF MANIA

Europe was not a great place to live in the 1500s. Most people were poor farmers, disease was rife, and the death rate was high. As if this were not enough, a great fear of witches, vampires, and werewolves swept across the continent. Between 1520 and 1630 over 30,000 people were reported to be werewolves in France alone. These fears could be put down to superstition and ignorance, but there might have been another reason. Many people at that time lived on a crop called rye. In wet areas, rye can be infected by ergot, a black fungus that contains a strong, mind-altering drug. When eaten, ergot can cause hallucinations—frightening imaginary visions that make it difficult for people to know what is real. Is it possible that some werewolf incidents were just visions caused by ergot poisoning?

Above *A werewolf runs amok devouring children while their terrified mother looks on in this 16th-century German engraving.*

NAVAJO SKINWALKERS

Shamans of the Navajo people of North America wear animal skins in order to take on those animals' powers and attributes. If they need strength, for instance, these "skinwalkers" will choose a bear; for cunning, a coyote. Unlike werewolves, whose animal side takes them over completely, skinwalkers' minds remain human. They might use special drugs, however, to help them to think like the creature. Some skinwalkers believe they actually transform into animals, others that the skin is just a mask.

Skinwalkers may use their ability for good or evil, so they should always be treated with caution. It's best not to stare them in the eye, as they can take on the form of another person by making eye contact with them!

Left *This Navajo shaman is wearing the skin of a bear.*

YETI AND SASQUATCH

High mountains and other wilderness areas provide the perfect refuge for all sorts of animals. But might they harbor something else? Could the vast, isolated Himalayan Mountains, for example, be hiding one of the world's most mysterious creatures—the yeti?

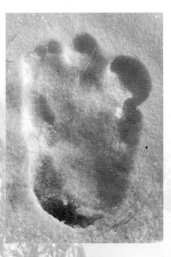

Left *One of the first photographs of a yeti footprint ever taken—this image shows an imprint 50 cm (1.5 ft) long.*

WILD MAN OF THE SNOWS

Explorer B.H. Hodgson couldn't believe his ears. It was 1832 and he was trekking through Nepal, in the soaring Himalayan Mountains, with local guides. One of them had just told him he had just seen a giant, hairy, two-legged creature loping ahead of them in the distance. The team investigated, but the creature had run away before they could get close enough to see it properly. After Hodgson reported the sighting, other explorers started coming back with similar stories about a large, ape-like creature and strange footprints in the snow.

The name "abominable snowman" was coined in 1921 by Charles Howard-Bury, who found footprints on an expedition to Mount Everest. His native guides told him the prints were made by a yeti, a "wild man of the snows." For years, the only evidence that this strange creature existed was eye-witness accounts, then in 1951 mountaineer Eric Shipton took photographs of a set of giant footprints. Could this be hard evidence

at last? The photographs sparked such an interest that a newspaper in the United Kingdom, the *Daily Mail,* mounted its own expedition to find out more. They discovered more footprints and tracked down a hairy scalp from a human-like creature, which was kept in a local monastery. Scientists carried out tests on the hair, but couldn't identify the animal it had come from. Since then there have been many more sightings, but no one has been able to catch this elusive animal or even take a photograph of it.

The discovery of fossils from a human-like species called *Homo floresiensis*, which lived in Indonesia only 16,000 years ago, has excited yeti watchers. If this human species existed so recently, who is to say that the yeti couldn't belong to another species similar to us that has survived to the present day, hidden from the rest of the world? We will only find out if further evidence is discovered.

APE MEN AROUND THE WORLD

In India, people talk of the nee-gued, a huge, man-like monster that lives in the mountains of Sikkim. The Tano Giant of Ghana, in West Africa, is a tall, two-legged creature with pale skin, black fur, an ape-like

BIGFOOT

If the yeti is the "wild man of the snow," then bigfoot, said to roam the remote valleys and forests in western Canada and the United States, is the "wild man of the woods." In fact the meaning of its other name, sasquatch—in the language of the Salish native people of British Columbia, Canada—means just that. Like the yeti, the sasquatch is shy and rarely seen. Reports of its appearance vary, but it is reckoned to be between 2–2½ meters (6.5–8 ft) tall with long arms, an ape-like face, a flat nose, and thick, dark brown or black hair all over its body. Again like the yeti, though various expeditions have set out to find it, the sasquatch has never been tracked down. Perhaps it's just as well. Apparently the creature stinks—a close encounter would probably be very unpleasant!

Above *This still from an amateur film of a bigfoot taken in 1967 has been revealed as a fake.*

head and no thumbs. Local people are terrified of the creature. They blame it for attacking people and even carrying them off. In Brazil and Paraguay a giant called a curinquean is said to kill cattle. Strangely, this man-monster likes to remove the animal's tongue, but leaves the rest of the body untouched.

Right *Local people reckon there are three types of giant man-creature living in the Himalayas. Of these yeti, or yeh-teh in Sherpa, is the smallest!*

GIANTS

Giant means "born of the earth" and giants certainly are man-mountains. Some giants are good, but a lot are bad; some are cunning, and others are stupid. Both kind and vicious giants feature here, in some of the popular giant tales—or "tall stories"—from around the world.

THE CYCLOPS

When the Greek hero Odysseus landed on the island of Sicily to gather supplies, he didn't know that the island was home to the cyclopes, terrifying one-eyed giants. Odysseus and his men took refuge in a cave where one of the cyclopes, Polyphemus, had made his home. Polyphemus kept sheep. Every evening he would drive his flock into the cave, and every morning he would let them out again to graze. When he returned that evening and discovered the men in his cave he was very angry. He ate two of them and trapped the rest by rolling a huge boulder across the entrance of the cave, intending to eat them one by one.

When the giant returned with his sheep the next evening, Odysseus tricked him into drinking wine and, while he was drunk, blinded him with the red-hot tip of an olive branch, which he had heated in the giant's fire. Despite his blindness, the cyclops tried to keep the men imprisoned, but they escaped the next morning by leaving the cave with the sheep. They fooled the giant by clinging on underneath the sheep, so he didn't know they were there.

THE SELFISH GIANT

A selfish giant, in a story by Irish writer Oscar Wilde, came home to his castle one day to find children playing in his garden. He was furious. He chased them away and forbade them from entering ever again. As a result of his meanness, it was winter in his garden for a long time. However, one day the children managed to break in. As they played, the snow melted and spring came to the garden at last —all except for one corner where it was still winter. In that corner, there was a little boy crying beneath a tall tree because he was too small to climb it. When the giant looked out his window and saw the little boy crying, his heart melted. He went out and lifted the child into the tree's branches, whereupon the boy hugged and kissed the huge giant. Immediately the snow disappeared and the tree burst into blossom.

From then on the giant loved having children play in his garden, but to his great sadness the little boy never came back. Many years passed. One day, in the depth of winter, when snow once again carpeted the garden, he saw the tree in the corner covered in white blossom. The little boy had come back! When the giant went out to the boy, the boy told him he had come to take the giant to live in his garden. The next day, when the children came to play, they found the giant dead, covered in white blossoms, beneath the same tree.

Right In "Jack and the Beanstalk," Jack plants a magic bean that grows into a massive beanstalk. Jack climbs it and finds a wicked but rich giant at the top. After several adventures, Jack steals the giant's gold and cuts down the beanstalk, sending the giant crashing to the ground.

DZOAVITS AND DOVE

In this Shoshone folk tale, from Nevada and Utah in the U.S.A., there was a terrifying giant called Dzoavits, who loved nothing better than to feast on the young of other animals. One day he stole two of Dove's eggs. Dove managed to get them back, but Dzoavits chased after her. Luckily, the other animals came to help her. Crane made a bridge with his leg so she could cross a river. Weasel dug escape tunnels for her. Eagle gave her some tallow, which turned into a great chasm, a stomach, which turned into a cliff, and some feathers, which became a thick mist, shielding her from the giant. But Dzoavits got past all these obstacles and was soon closing in on her again.

Finally, Badger made a hole where Dove and her children could hide. He then dug a second hole and told Dzoavits she was in that one. When the giant stormed into it, Badger threw burning rocks down after him and sealed him in. And there he remains to this day—unless the hole erupts into a volcano and releases him.

Right Odysseus and his men drive a burning stake into the single eye of the giant cyclops.

OGRES AND TROLLS

Mean, ugly, and stupid, ogres and trolls are not nice to know. They tend to be bigger than people and have a taste for human flesh. Thankfully, ogres and trolls can usually be outwitted by clever humans.

The word "ogre" was first used by French fairy-tale writers over 300 years ago to describe any bad-tempered, lumbering, human-like beast, and since then ogres of one sort or another have clumped their way into folklore from Russia to Africa and from Japan to Canada. Fearsome trolls from Sweden, Finland, and Norway might be as huge as giants or as small as dwarves. Whatever their size, both trolls and ogres are renowned for their terrible ugliness, and if the stories are anything to go by, they have ugly personalities to match.

OGRES

Ogres go by many different names, but they all have one thing in common—stupidity. Take, for example, the ogre who fell in love with the reflection of a beautiful girl in a lake and drank the lake dry to try and get her! In a tale from Kenya, an ogre wants to eat a girl he has captured but lets her choose where she will be cooked and what type of leaves he will cook her in. The girl cleverly takes a long time to make the decisions, giving her warrior boyfriend enough time to find her and kill the ogre. Oni are hideous Japanese ogres with horns, sharp claws, wild hair, and red or blue skin.

Left *This enormous ogre has brought home three cows for his wife. She doesn't look very pleased to receive this gruesome gift!*

They usually carry a heavy club and like to eat humans. Every spring villages across Japan perform a special ceremony to keep these vile spirits away. The Ojibway people of the U.S.A. and Canada scare their children with stories of the terrifying Wendigo, another monstrous ogre that likes to eat people!

Left In the film Shrek, the main character is an ogre—but he is a misunderstood creature, who just wants to live a quiet life in his swampy home.

TROLLS

Like ogres, trolls are truly hideous in appearance, but their womenfolk can sometimes be beautiful, with long red hair. Trolls live underground, making their homes deep inside hills and mountains. They come out at night to hunt—indulging in an unhealthy liking for human flesh. If they come out into the open during the day, however, sunlight will turn them into stone. Trolls are excellent metalworkers and are also hoarders of treasure. The trolls of the Inuit people of northern Canada are huge and hairy and have long, knife-like fingernails and massive stomachs that drag on the ground.

Right In the Norwegian folktale illustrated here, a hero peasant named Askeladden (or Ash Lad) gets the better of a rather stupid troll.

BEAUTY AND THE BEAST

In this French fairy tale, a traveling merchant stumbles across a castle hidden in a forest. When he plucks a single rosebud from the garden for his daughter, Belle, the owner of the castle, a terrible ogre, catches him. The beast demands that the merchant hands over his daughter as punishment for the theft. Belle settles into life at the castle, growing to enjoy the ogre's company. Eventually, however, she becomes homesick. The ogre agrees to let her go home as long as she returns in a week. He gives her a magic mirror and a ring to take with her. Belle's sisters persuade her to stay longer than the week, but Belle is horrified when she looks in the mirror and sees the Beast lying heartbroken beneath the rosebush. She uses the magic ring to transport herself back to the castle. When she finds only the Beast's lifeless body, she cries bitterly and declares her love for him. As her tears wash over him, the Beast revives and miraculously transforms into a handsome prince. He tells her that he had been enchanted by a wicked fairy and that her love has finally broken the terrible curse.

MONSTROUS WOMEN

Imagine a monster so terrifyingly hideous that taking a single glance at her face would turn you into stone. Medusa the gorgon, with her snake hair and pointed tusks, was one such horror. Like many of the most frightening creatures from Greek myths, Medusa was female. Read on to meet her sisters and some other hair-raising women.

THE GORGONS

Medusa was one of three beautiful sisters, but she angered the goddess Athena, who turned them into three snake-haired monsters called gorgons. They sprouted leathery wings and bronze claws and grew huge tusks from their gaping mouths, causing their tongues to loll out in a sickening fashion. Just to look at their terrible faces was enough to turn you to stone. Horrified by their own appearance, this grim trio hid away in an underground lair near the entrance to the Underworld (the home of the dead) guarded by their three other, equally revolting sisters, the Grey Ones. These withered old hags had only one eye and one tooth between them, which they shared. Their Greek names—Deino, Enyo, and Pemphredo—translate as "dread," "horror," and "beware."

Right *Just one glimpse of the hideous, snake-haired head of Medusa the gorgon was enough to turn the unfortunate onlooker to stone.*

HARPIES

Evil-smelling and vicious, the harpies were vile crones with the wings, tails, and talons of vultures. They lived on an island and attacked any ships that came their way, snatching the men on board and devouring them. Two of these monstrous creatures were sent by the gods to torment Phineas, a seer who could foretell the future. The gods were angry because his prophecies kept coming true. The harpies blinded Phineas to punish him, but they didn't stop there. They swooped down onto his table at every meal, covering the food with their foul droppings or carrying it away in their claws. In the end, the flying nightmares were finally chased away by two sons of the North Wind and turned into whirlwinds.

Left *Harpy means "snatcher," and these winged daughters of the sea god Thaumas would swoop down and snatch anything that took their fancy.*

PERSEUS AND MEDUSA

There was once a king called Polydectes who fell in love with the beautiful Danae. But Danae didn't want to marry him. The king agreed to leave Danae in peace if her son, Perseus, would bring back the head of Medusa the gorgon—a task the king hoped would be impossible and lead to Perseus's death. The gorgons were hidden deep inside a labyrinth of underground tunnels guarded by their sisters, the Grey Ones. Luckily for Perseus the gods decided to help him. They gave him a shield, a helmet, a sickle, and a pair of winged sandals.

Perseus used the sandals to fly to the gorgons' lair. To get past the Grey Ones he put on the helmet, which made him invisible. He found the vile hags passing their single eye between them, so he grabbed it off them and wouldn't give it back until they told him where to find the gorgons. They directed him down the maze of tunnels where he eventually found the hideous sisters sleeping. Instead of facing her directly, Perseus crept up on Medusa, looking only at her reflection in his polished shield. He struck her head from her body with the sickle, and as her blood hit the ground Pegasus, the winged horse, sprang from it. Perseus grabbed Medusa's head, shoved it into a sack, and leapt onto Pegasus' back. He flew back to Polydectes, pulled the head from the sack, and turned the king to stone, freeing his mother at last.

MEN OF WOOD AND FOREST

Look deep into the heart of the forest—vast and unexplored, it is a place of darkness, magic, and mystery. Woodland beings, part man and part spirit, are said to dwell among the trees in myths and stories from all over the world: sometimes they control nature; sometimes nature controls them. Always be careful when you venture into shady groves …

The strange face of a man made up entirely of leaves stares out from carvings on medieval buildings, particularly churches, all across Europe. But this mysterious figure, the Green Man, is nothing to do with Christianity. He is much, much older. His image appears in temples in Mesopotamia (Iraq) that were built thousands of years ago. He can also be seen on ancient buildings in India and Thailand. The Green Man is the spirit of nature. He can bring rain and ensure that plants grow. In European folklore, he dies in the winter to be reborn again in the spring. Traditional May Day festivals, which echo ancient pagan festivities that took place on the first of May, celebrate the Green Man even today.

THE BOKWUS

A far less pleasant creature than the Green Man from European folklore haunts the larch and spruce forests of North America: the Bokwus, the silent guardian of every woodland, whose face is only ever glimpsed between the leaves. Although also a green man of the woods, the Bokwus is no friend to humans. Travelers passing through the woods should take particular care near running water. The Bokwus may well try to push them in, so he can take their souls as they are drowning and take them back to his forest home.

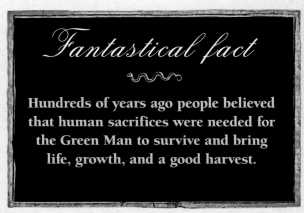

Fantastical fact

Hundreds of years ago people believed that human sacrifices were needed for the Green Man to survive and bring life, growth, and a good harvest.

Left *The Green Man, also known as Jack-in-the-Green, Green Jack, Green George, or The Leaf King, welcomes in the summer during May Morning revels in an English village.*

Right The old man of the woods: this image brings out the unearthly side of the strange Green Man.

HERNE THE HUNTER

Riding through the woods at breakneck speed, hounds baying at his heels, the specter of Herne the Hunter is a terrifying sight. Leading a ghostly hunt on his jet-black horse, with huge antlers growing from his head, Herne haunts the woodlands of Windsor Great Park in southern England. He is said to have been the chief huntsman to a medieval king, Richard II. He once saved the king's life when Richard was attacked by white stag. Herne threw himself in the path of the stag and received a terrible wound that nearly killed him. He recovered with the help of a wizard, but at a price: the wizard took away his hunting skills. In despair, Herne hanged himself from an oak tree in Windsor Great Park, at that time a huge forest. His uneasy spirit has haunted the same place ever since.

Below Ghostly Herne the Hunter leads a night-time hunt through Windsor Great Park.

HORNED AND HOOFED CREATURES

Fantastical horses take many forms in the world's myths and folklore. There is Pegasus, the winged horse of the ancient Greeks, and there is the pure and innocent unicorn of medieval belief, whose horn could neutralize poison. Ireland, Scotland, and Scandinavia have their demonic water horses, who whisk the unwary away on their backs. The wild centaurs of Greek and Roman myth are unpredictable beasts; half-man, half-horse, and prone to violent outbursts, though some are wise and have the gift of prophecy. Other human-beast hybrids that feature in Greek and Roman tales include the fearsome man-bull the Minotaur and satyrs, with cloven hooves and horns. In the language of symbols, the animal part represents the fiercer and wilder side of human nature.

North America

Atlantic Ocean

South America

1 Ireland
The playful pooka

2 Scotland
Kelpies, malicious water horses; each uisgé

3 Shetland
Neugle, a water horse

4 Isle of Man
Glashtyn, a water horse

5 Scandinavia
Eight-legged Sleipnir, nickur water horses

6 Europe
Unicorns

7 Japan
Kirin, the gentle eastern unicorn

8 China
Qilin, the Chinese unicorn

9 Tibet
Serou, tsopou, and kere, fierce unicorns

10 Mongolia
Poh, the tiger-devouring unicorn

11 Middle East
Kujata, Arzshenk

12 Greece
Half-man, half-bull Minotaur; winged Pegasus; half-goat, half-man satyrs; half-man, half-horse centaurs

13 Italy
Gentle, goat-like fauns

14 North America
Thunderhorses

15 Egypt
Ptah, the Apis bull

Arctic Ocean

③
⑤
②
①④
⑥ Europe

Asia

⑬ ⑫

⑮

Africa

⑪

⑩

⑧

⑨

⑦

Pacific Ocean

Indian Ocean

Australia

N
W   E
S

UNICORNS

The beautiful and magical unicorn is a mystical horse with a single spiral horn growing from its forehead. Unicorns of Japan and China are gentle creatures, but beware the kere of Tibet—this unicorn has a vicious temper.

Over 2,000 years ago, an Egyptian scholar wrote the first known description of a unicorn. According to him it was a very colorful animal that looked like a large, wild ass (donkey) with a long red, white, and black horn, a purple head, and blue eyes—quite a combination! This unicorn was very fierce and thought nothing of attacking elephants. The Roman writer Pliny the Elder said the unicorn was like a horse with elephant's feet and a deer's head. Marco Polo, a medieval adventurer who traveled from Italy to China and saw many weird and wonderful things along the way, described a very ugly unicorn with elephant's feet, a boar's head, a single black horn, and a habit of wallowing in mud—this was almost certainly a rhinoceros!

Left *Unlike all other fantastic beasts, the unicorn has no dark side—it is good, selfless, and beautiful and cannot be captured by force but only by gentleness.*

Magical powers of a unicorn horn

The horn of the unicorn is supposed to have magical properties, including the power to:

- Heal
- Cure and protect against disease
- Whiten teeth
- Raise the dead
- Detect poison
- Purify water

The traditional image of a unicorn is of a pure-white, horse-like creature with a lion's tail, cloven hooves, a curled white beard, and a long, spiral horn. This understanding of unicorns probably began when Bible stories were mixed with other tales about one-horned beasts. In the tales that were created from this blend, the unicorn is a shy, wild animal that lives in the forest. It can only be captured when a pure and beautiful maiden lures it from hiding. The unicorn will rest its head in the girl's lap and go to sleep, from that moment becoming tame.

ALICORN

Unicorn horn, which was given the name "alicorn," was one of the rarest and most expensive materials in the world in medieval times, worth many times its weight in gold. Alicorns were given as gifts between kings and queens and the wealthy, especially people with enemies who might want to kill them. These people made cups out of them to drink from, as alicorns were said to have the power to neutralize any poison. All of the items that were once thought to be made of alicorn we now know were made from the long, spiral tusk of the narwhal, a small whale that lives in the northern part of the Atlantic Ocean.

UNICORNS OF THE EAST

China and Japan have their own unicorns. The qilin of China was first mentioned in stories 5,000 years ago, when it sprang from the Yellow River to appear before a sage (a very wise man). The qilin has a deer's body, a lion's head, and a single, curved horn and is covered in green scales. It is very pure, has the perfect balance of yin and yang (two opposite natural forces), and combines all the elements (earth, fire, water, wood, and metal). To see a qilin is a good omen but they appear very rarely and only to wise and good people or at the birth or death of someone very important. The qilin is the most powerful creature in Chinese mythology after the dragon and the phoenix. Despite this unicorn's power, it is extremely gentle; it can walk on grass without crushing it and will avoid stepping on insects for fear of killing them. In Japan, the unicorn is called a kirin and to see one is a sign of good luck. The kirin can tell the truth from lies: it punishes the wicked by running them through with its horn; but rewards those who are good by protecting them and granting them good luck.

Not quite so gentle is the poh of Mongolia. This is a fierce creature with claws, sharp fangs, a long horn, and a black tail. It preys on leopards and tigers and has a terrible howl! In mountainous Tibet lurk the serou, the tsopou, and the kere. Little is known of these unicorns except that they are hostile and should not be approached.

Right *This sculpture of a qilin from the Summer Palace in Beijing, China, sports two horns.*

PEGASUS

Pegasus is one of the most beautiful creatures in the myths of the ancient Greeks. This gentle, giant, winged horse is also the only fantastic creature in Greek mythology that is wholly good. Two Greek heroes, Perseus and Bellerophon, rode Pegasus, and he also served Zeus, the king of the gods.

THE STORY OF PEGASUS

When the Greek hero Perseus slew the vile gorgon Medusa (see page 68), a winged horse, Pegasus, sprang from her blood as it spurted from her severed neck onto the ground. Pegasus served Perseus until the day Perseus died, then he was caught by the goddess Athene and sent to the home of the Muses. These nine goddesses of the arts and sciences relied on a magical spring of water to give them inspiration, but the spring had dried up. When Pegasus stamped his hoof, a new source of water called the Hippocrene spring emerged from the ground.

Pegasus next served the hero Bellerophon, a brave warrior sent by King Iobates to kill the Chimera, a hideous beast laying waste to the country. Bellerophon prayed to Athena for help and she gave him a golden bridle. The next day Bellerophon found Pegasus drinking at a spring and the magical horse allowed Bellerophon to put the bridle on him and ride him. Mounted on Pegasus, Bellerophon easily defeated the Chimera, soaring down upon it and thrusting a spear down its throat, killing it instantly. King Iobates gave Bellerophon his daughter in marriage, but this was not enough for proud Bellerophon. He thought he could fly on Pegasus up to the top of Mount Olympus, the home of the gods, and become one of them, so he set out, leaving his wife behind. Zeus, the king of the gods, decided to punish him for such impudence and sent a stinging gadfly to attack Pegasus.

Above *Bellerophon, astride Pegasus, swoops down on the chimera, a terrifying female monster.*

When the fly stung him, Pegasus bucked and reared in pain, throwing Bellerophon down to Earth. Bellerophon didn't die but was blinded and crippled and doomed to wander aimlessly in the wilderness for the rest of his life.

Zeus kept Pegasus to carry his thunderbolts for him and Pegasus was also ridden by the goddess of the dawn, Eos. Eventually Pegasus took a mate, and their offspring began a race of winged horses. On the last day of his life, Zeus honored Pegasus by turning him into a constellation of stars in the night sky. As he flew up to the heavens, a single feather from one of his wings fell to Earth near the city of Tarsus.

Above *Pegasus was the magical steed of Greek heroes Bellerophon and Perseus and served both faithfully.*

CHIMERA

The chimera was a terrifying, fire-breathing monster with the head and body of a lion, a goat's head sprouting from her back, and a living, writhing serpent for a tail. No one had been able to defeat this monster, as they could not get close enough without being seared by her fiery breath. But on Pegasus's back, Bellerophon could fly out of range and still aim his spear down at her. The metal tip of the spear entered her throat and melted in the heat there, choking her to death.

WATER HORSES

If you see a bewitching horse on the banks of a river or lake, or if a horse seems to be calling your name, think twice before you go anywhere near it. This could be a mischievous, shape-shifting fairy that likes nothing better than to lure you onto its back and take you on a breakneck ride. There's no telling where you might end up!

Water horses feature in the folk stories of many northern European countries. They go by different names in different places, and some are more dangerous than others. Anyone rash enough to agree to a ride on an Irish pooka could be sure they were in for a wild ride, but the Scottish kelpie is an even more dangerous proposition. Anyone unfortunate enough to come across a kelpie is unlikely to survive unscathed.

THE POOKA

The pooka of Ireland often appears as a restless and mischievous horse—sleek and black, with a flowing mane and tail and yellow eyes. He will call anyone who offends him to come and ride with him. If they refuse, he will go on a destructive rampage, storming across the countryside, tearing through hedges and demolishing gates and fences. The pooka might dive into water and give his rider a drenching or throw him into a muddy ditch. Some say there is an even darker side to the pooka. When he haunts wild, watery places he can be very dangerous—especially to children. If they are tempted to ride him, he is likely to carry them off over a cliff and kill them. The pooka is a wily shape-shifter and will sometimes appear as a goat, dog, goblin, or even an eagle rather than a horse. The pooka can, however, be helpful to those in need. He has been known to work in the fields for poor farmers and even to help with chores around the house.

Above *The mischievous pooka will take its unwary rider on a wild ride that usually ends up in a severe drenching!*

KELPIE

Like the pooka, the kelpie is a shape-shifter that usually appears as a wild horse. This evil fairy, which haunts the rivers and streams of Scotland and is often seen draped in dank waterweed, lures the unwary onto its back then dives into the nearest water, where it will drown and devour its victims. The kelpie is jet-black or occasionally white, with water dripping constantly from its mane and tail. Its skin is deathly cold to the touch. Kelpies are creatures of fresh and running water, so it is possible to escape from one by crossing a body of still or stagnant water, such as a muddy puddle. In human form kelpies are often ugly and squat with pointed ears, big teeth, and seaweed for hair. They can make themselves handsome, but they can never get rid of all the seaweed in their hair.

A similar phantom is the each uisgé, which makes its home in saltwater lochs (lakes) and in the sea around Ireland and Scotland. It appears as an ugly, shaggy colt. If anyone touches an each uisgé their hands will stick to its hide so they cannot let go, and they will then be dragged, helpless, into the water. The each uisgé eats both humans and animals, tearing their bodies apart but always leaving the liver untouched.

Right *A kelpie emerges menacingly from the depths of its watery lair, ready to seek out its next unfortunate victim.*

NORTHERN WATER HORSES

There are also tales of water horses in Scandinavia and the Shetland Islands of Scotland. The nickur of Scandinavia has hooves that face backwards and can also appear as a boy, a centaur, or a green-bearded old man. In their human form, nickurs sometimes fall in love with mortal women. They can be found in any watery place and like to be left alone to make music, so be careful not to disturb one or it will drown you without hesitating. Fishermen in the far north always keep a knife made of iron in the bottom of the boat, a weapon that is known to ward off nickurs.

In Shetland, the neugle lives in the water and is terrified of fire. It looks like a pretty, gray pony with a green mane and a wheel-shaped tail arching over its back. Anyone who dares to ride it will get dragged beneath the waters, which will light up with blue flames as the neugle slides below them.

THE MINOTAUR

The Greek myth of Theseus and the Minotaur has everything: a brave and handsome hero, a clever and beautiful heroine, a terrifying monster, love, action, horror, betrayal, and a strange love affair between a queen and a bull!

THESEUS AND THE MINOTAUR

Things started going wrong for Minos, King of Crete (an island in the Mediterranean Sea), when he kept a gift of a beautiful white bull for himself instead of sacrificing it to Poseidon, god of the sea. Poseidon decided on an unusual punishment for Minos: he made the king's wife fall in love with the bull! The result of this odd love match was that the queen gave birth to the hideous Minotaur, with the body of a man but the head and tail of a bull. Worse then this, the monster acquired a taste for human flesh. Horrified, King Minos shut the poor beast away in the Labyrinth, a vast maze of tunnels he had built beneath his palace. But he had to keep the monster fed.

Minos solved this problem by demanding that Athens, a city across the sea that owed him a tribute (a payment made from one state to another), should send seven young men and seven young women every nine years to be offered to the Minotaur. They were to be locked into the Labyrinth, where they would wander the tunnels until they were eventually found and devoured. When it was time for the third shipment of young Athenians to Crete, the prince of Athens, a brave young man called Theseus, decided he would go with them and kill the Minotaur. His father, the king, was worried. He told Theseus that if he succeeded, he must fly white sails on his boat when he returned, so the king would know all was well. If he failed, the ship should fly black sails.

When the Athenians arrived in Crete, Theseus met King Minos's daughter Ariadne, who fell in love with Theseus and offered to help him if he promised to take her with him. She gave him a ball of golden twine, explaining that he should tie one end to the gate at the entrance to the Labyrinth and unravel it as he made his way through the

THESEVS SLAYS THE MINOTAVR

Left *Using King Minos's sword, given to him by Ariadne, Theseus ends the Minotaur's reign of terror for good.*

*maze. By following
it back again he
would be able to
find his way out.
She also gave him a
sword. The next day,
Theseus did exactly
as she had instructed
him. Deep inside the
Labyrinth he found
the Minotaur sleeping.
As Theseus approached,
the murderous beast
awoke and charged, but
Theseus was ready. He slew
the Minotaur with a single
sword-stroke, followed the thread
back to safety, and escaped to his ship
with Ariadne and the other Athenians.*

*On the voyage home, they stopped at
the island of Naxos. While they were there
something happened between Theseus and
Ariadne and he sailed away without her.
The gods wanted to punish Theseus for
abandoning Ariadne, so Zeus made him
forget his promise to his father, King
Aegeus—to use the white sails if he
succeeded. When the king saw the
ship returning with black sails
flying, he thought Theseus had
failed. Overcome with grief, he
hurled himself into the sea. Ever
since then, that particular part
of the Mediterranean has been
known as the Aegean Sea.*

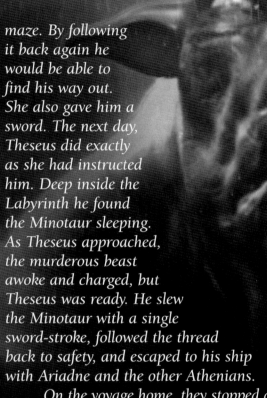

SACRED BULLS

Bulls are strong, impressive, and powerful beasts, so it's
not surprising that they crop up in many myths and
legends. In Islamic myths, Kujata is a colossal bull with
4,000 eyes, ears, noses, and legs! He has an enormous
ruby on his back, on top of which stands an angel,
supporting the world on its shoulders. In the Zoroastrian
religion of ancient Persia Arzshenk, a bull-headed monster
like the Minotaur, was the king of demons. He was finally
slain by the hero Rustam after a mammoth battle that
lasted many days. To the ancient Egyptians the bull
was the most important of all sacred animals. A
series of magnificent bullocks were chosen to be
the living embodiment of the god Ptah. Each was
worshiped and honored until the age of 28, when
it was ritually sacrificed, mummified, and buried
with great ceremony and mourning.

Left *The magnificent Apis, shown here on an ancient
limestone slab, was a bull god worshiped in ancient Egypt.*

CENTAURS

Half-human and half-horse, the centaur is another fabulous creature that originated in the Greek myths. Some centaurs, such as the noble Chiron, were scholarly and wise, but many were wild and unruly, causing havoc wherever they went.

Above *A centaur prepared for battle in the 2005 film about Narnia, The Lion the Witch and the Wardrobe.*

CENTAURS IN CHILDREN'S STORIES

Just like the centaurs in the Greek myths, centaurs in the Harry Potter stories are wild beings that live in the dark depths of the forest, but they are not as brutal as the centaurs of myth. Some are helpful to humans (and wizards); others are not. They also have the gift of prophecy, being able to foretell the future from looking at the stars. In the Narnia stories by C.S. Lewis, centaurs ally themselves with the sons and daughters of Adam (humans) against the forces of evil. They are wise and brave creatures that are skilled in battlecraft. Lewis's centaurs also have the gift of prophecy and some are great healers.

Centaurs would definitely not have made good neighbors. These creatures, with the head, chest, and arms of a man and the body and legs of a horse, were wild and brutal. They ate raw flesh and were constantly getting drunk, running riot, trampling crops, and attacking anyone who got in their way. They weren't very bright, either, though some were cunning and wily. The centaurs lived in great herds on Mount Pelion, in the Thessaly region of northeastern Greece.

Zeus, the king of the gods, would often get centaurs to do his dirty work—particularly punishing anyone who had annoyed him. This led to a lot of bad feeling between centaurs and humans. On one occasion, a group of centaurs ran amok at a wedding sparking a massive battle.

Not all centaurs were so wild. The centaur Chiron was immortal and one of the wisest beings ever to live, being skilled in hunting, medicine, music, and prophecy. He was so learned that the gods put him in charge of educating some of the greatest Greek heroes, such as Hercules, Jason, and Achilles. Sadly, Chiron got caught up in the conflict between the centaurs and humans at the wedding battle, fighting on the side of the men, and was injured by a poisoned arrow. Because he was immortal, the wound didn't kill him, but the poison meant he was doomed to live in agony forever. Zeus took

HERCULES AND NESSUS

Hercules was one of the greatest Greek heroes. One day, not long after he had married a beautiful girl called Deianeira, the centaur Nessus offered to ferry them across a wide river that they had to cross. Nessus set off with Deianeira first, but he was not to be trusted and tried to abduct her. Hercules chased after him and shot him with a poisoned arrow. Before he died, Nesses told Deianeira to take some of his blood and keep it. If she ever thought Hercules was being unfaithful, the centaur told her, the blood would restore his love for her.

Deianera kept the phial of blood for many years, until she heard rumours that Hercules had fallen in love with another woman. She smeared some of the blood on a shirt and sent it to Hercules. When he put on the shirt, the blood, still tainted by the arrow's poison, burnt into his flesh—in agony, Hercules threw himself onto a fire and died. Nessus had got his revenge.

pity on him and allowed him to die, afterwards placing his body in the heavens as the constellation Sagittarius.

Above Nessus abducts Deianeira and is shot by Hercules, who is unaware that the same arrow will later be the cause of his own death.

THE SIOUX THUNDERHORSE

In the myths of the Lakota Sioux people of North America, thunderhorses are bringers of storms. They gallop across the sky, carrying on their backs warriors with lightning sticks. The thunder you hear during storms is the pounding of their hooves. Stories about giant horses probably started when people found fossil bones from an extinct, rhinoceros-like animal now known as a Brontothere. Standing over 2 meters (6.5 ft) tall at the shoulder and at least 4 meters (13 ft) long, these giants had long, horse-like faces and flattened horns on their noses.

SATYRS

Wild creatures of the woods, satyrs are half-man and half-goat. In Greek myths they are servants of Dionysus, god of wine, and like nothing better than a drunken party. Their counterparts in Roman myths, fauns, are similar to look at but completely different in character. They are gentle, peaceable forest creatures with a love of music.

With their pointed ears, strange animal-like features, horns, muscular bodies, and goats' legs and hooves, satyrs were definitely more animal than human. Although they were bold when it came to dancing, partying, drinking, feasting, and chasing beautiful nymphs, satyrs were also idle and cowardly—they never did any work and would run away at the first sign of trouble. Unlike many mythical creatures, satyrs were mortal, growing old and eventually dying, as humans do. Older satyrs were called sileni, and their leader was Silenus, a drunken, grizzled being often seen riding on a donkey. Silenus and the satyrs were the companions of Dionysus, joining him in drunken revels at every opportunity. Satyrs posed no serious threat to humans, but they were known as pranksters and could be rude and obnoxious.

In the myths of the Romans, fauns were similar creatures to satyrs. They had the legs and horns of goat and the torso, head, and feet of a man. They were the guardians of fields and forests. The gentle Mr Tumnus, who was a character in C.S. Lewis's book about Narnia, *The Lion, the Witch and the Wardrobe*, was a faun.

Above Fun-loving satyrs frolic with nymphs in the haze of the early morning. Satyrs were well known for their love of music, revelry, and dancing.

Above Pan plays his syrinx pipes—now commonly known as pan pipes—among the reeds on the banks of a quiet river.

THE GOD PAN

Pan was the son of the god Hermes and the nymph Dryope. He looked much like a satyr, with the legs, tail, hooves, and horns of a goat and the body of a man. His role was to guard flocks—sheep and goats. Although wild and fun loving, Pan also loved art and music. He was often to be heard playing the pipes.

One of the famous tales about Pan is the story of how he got his pan pipes. One day he came across Syrinx, a beautiful nymph who was beloved by all the satyrs, though she scorned them all. When she came face to face with Pan she ran from him, but he chased after her and caught up with her at the bank of a river. She called on the help of her fellow river nymphs. They turned her into a reed and turned into reeds themselves, swaying softly in the breeze. As the wind blew through them, it created a gentle melody. Although he could no longer recognize the object of his desire, Pan took some of the reeds and made them into pipes. He called his instrument a "syrinx" in her honor.

Above Mr Tumnus the faun as he appeared in the first of the Chronicles of Narnia films, based on C.S. Lewis's famous books.

DRAGONS

Appearing in legends all over the world, dragons are creatures of great power and magic. Some can fly, their great wings beating against their scaly sides; others lurk in caves guarding hoards of treasure, ready to emerge and belch forth a plume of fire. The traditional western image of a dragon is perhaps best shown by the fire-breathing beast famously killed by Saint George in Libya, North Africa. But dragons come in all shapes and sizes. Mayan and Aztec god Quetzalcoatl was a huge, feathered, flying serpent. In China and Japan, most dragons were bearded creatures that could not fly, and some were very small; while in Europe, many dragons were wingless, cave-dwelling "worms." In the myths of the ancient Greeks dragons were many-headed monsters with poison running in their veins.

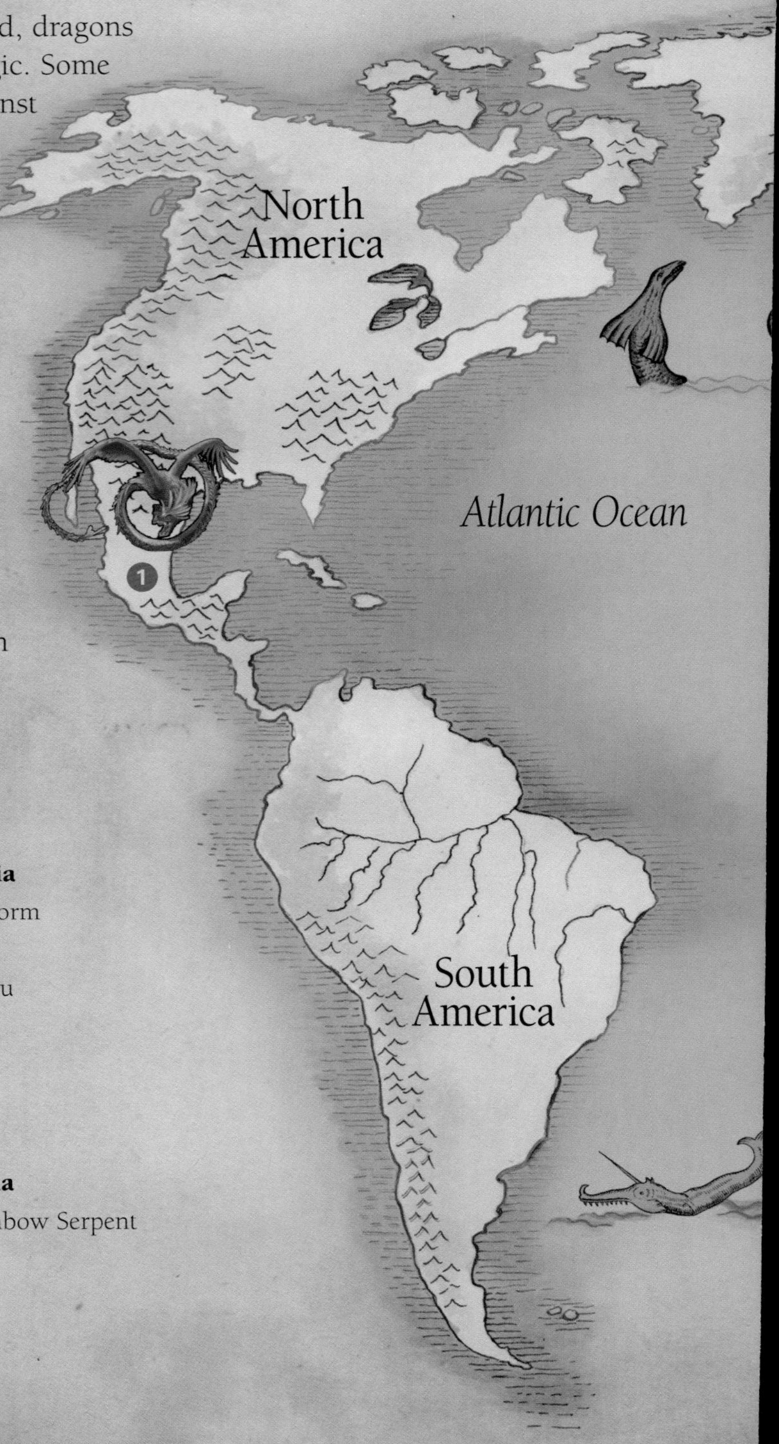

North America

Atlantic Ocean

South America

❶ Mexico and Central America
Quetzalcoatl—the plumed serpent

❷ Wales
The Red Dragon

❸ England
Winged, fire-breathing dragons

❹ Europe
Worms

❺ Scandanavia
Fafnir

❻ Greece
Many-headed dragons Ladon and Hydra

❼ China
Lung, including imperial dragons

❽ Mongolia
Death worm

❾ Japan
Tatsu, ryu

❿ Egypt
Apophis

⓫ Mali
Bida

⓬ Australia
The Rainbow Serpent

Arctic Ocean

Europe

Asia

Africa

Pacific Ocean

Indian Ocean

Australia

DRAGON LORE

"The dragon is the largest of all serpents and of all living things on Earth—not even the elephant is safe from the dragon," wrote a dragon observer some 1,500 years ago. In many parts of the world dragons are the most terrifying of all fantastic beasts, but in other places they are seen as gentle creatures, god-like and wise.

Above *Dragon-like Quetzalcoatl was believed by ancient peoples of Central America to be the creator of humankind.*

With their huge size, scaly skin, leathery wings, razor-sharp teeth and claws, and the ability to breathe fire, dragons are often regarded as the ultimate monster. In many ancient cultures dragons were thought to be evil. The Egyptian dragon, Apophis, for example, was the deadly enemy of the sun god, Ra. In Central America, a feathered serpent called Quetzalcoatl was a great god, while in India dragons were giant snakes—sometimes kindly, sometimes not. African dragons have a taste for human sacrifices: the snake-like Bida of Mali ate ten girls every year until his head was cut off by the hero Mamadi. In the East, dragons are viewed

THE RED DRAGON OF WALES

A fiery red dragon is the national emblem of Wales and relates to a legend about the wizard Merlin when he was just a boy. About 1,500 years ago, King Vortigern of the Britons was trying to build a great fortress in Wales to defend himself against the invading Saxons. But every time his builders laid the foundations, they were mysteriously destroyed. Vortigern consulted his magicians, who said he needed to sacrifice a boy with no father and sprinkle his blood on the ground. They searched the length and breadth of the country for such a boy, until they found a lad called Myrddin Emrys (Merlin), whose father was said to be a demon, and brought him before Vortigern. When the king's magicians explained what kept happening, Myrddin laughed. He told them that beneath the ground there was a vast pool where two battling dragons lived, one red and one white. The fighting of these great beasts was causing the ground to shake and bringing the walls of Vortigern's fortress crashing to the ground.

differently. Chinese, Japanese, and Korean dragons are considered to be god-like and are usually friendly towards people.

DRAGON BONES?

No-one knows where dragon stories came from, but they might have developed from a fear of snakes. In Australia, for example, tales of the Rainbow Serpent, a fearsome but respected figure in Aboriginal mythology, may have come from encounters with a gigantic, 15-meter-long (50 ft) snake called *Wonambi naracoortensi*. This reptilian giant became extinct shortly after humans settled in Australia, about 50,000 years ago. Even if people never saw the snake itself, they could have seen its fossilized bones.

Below *Dragons feature in the creation stories of many cultures, from Central America to Iraq. Sometimes they are kind, but in the Bible dragons are described as the servants of Satan.*

89

Chinese Dragons

The dragon is the most important of all the legendary creatures of China. Dragons are like gods, having power over weather, fire, and water. They are worshiped as symbols of power and happiness and thought to bring with them wealth and good luck.

I n China dragons are called *lung* or *long* and live for thousands of years. Unlike most western dragons, they are generally kind towards humans. Their physical characteristics are also distinctive. They have snake-like bodies, 4 legs, and 117 scales covering their bodies. They live for thousands of years and very old dragons may eventually grow wings. You will often see Chinese dragons shown carrying a pearl in their mouth, claws, or under their chin. This represents their power. Most Chinese dragons have four claws on each foot, apart from imperial dragons, which have five.

According to Chinese legend, the farther a dragon travels away from China, the more claws it loses. This explains why dragons from Korea have four claws while those from Japan have only three. Another legend describes how Huang Lung, the yellow dragon, gave humans the gift of writing. One day, he rose up out of the Yellow River before the Emperor Fu Xi and showed him characters that were written along his flanks.

The Mongolian Death Worm

Although not exactly a dragon, the death worm of Mongolia is a terrifying and mysterious snake-like animal. It is a cryptozoological creature; that is, an animal that may or may not be real. There have been sightings of the death worm, but its actual existence has not been scientifically proven. The worm is supposed to live

underground in the vast Gobi Desert of Mongolia, north of China. It grows up to 1½ meters (5 ft) long and is smooth, fat, and blood red! Its local name is Allghoi Khorkhoi, which means "blood-filled intestine worm." Local people say it can spit deadly sulfuric acid and kill its prey from a distance with a bolt of electricity. Some zoologists (scientists who study animals) have been so intrigued by tales of the frightening creature that in 2005 an expedition set out for Mongolia to try and track it down. Unfortunately, no trace of the scarlet worm was found—the mystery remains.

Above *The death worm's Mongolian name means "blood-filled intestine worm." This is one artist's vision of the creature.*

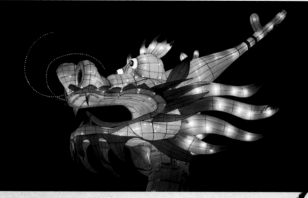

Left Huge paper dragons— symbols of luck and prosperity— are often paraded around the streets at Chinese new year.

YEAR OF THE DRAGON

In Chinese astrology, each year has its own particular zodiac animal. There are twelve in all: rat, monkey, horse, tiger, snake, ox, horse, sheep, rooster, dog, pig, and dragon—the dragon being the only mythical creature. Because the Chinese New Year starts at the end of January or the beginning of February, the zodiac years span two calendar years. Dragon years in the last half century have been: 1964–65, 1976–77, 1988–89, and 2000–2001. The next year of the dragon will be 2012–13. Anyone born in the year of the dragon is said to be lively, strong, and attractive, but these people can also be ruthless, stopping at nothing to get what they want.

Number of dragons

Nine is a magical number in China and features strongly in Chinese dragon myths. Dragons are said to be made up of the following nine parts:

- Head of a camel
- Neck and body of a snake
- Antlers of a deer
- Eyes of a rabbit
- Ears of a bull
- Belly of a clam
- Scales of a fish
- Claws of an eagle
- Paws of a tiger

Above This is an example of a five-toed imperial dragon. Did you know that the greatest compliment you could pay the Chinese Emperor was to call him "Dragon Face?"

JAPANESE DRAGONS

Japan is a beautiful country with many tall mountains, deep lakes, and dark forests. It's easy to believe that mystical creatures, such as dragons, might dwell in some of the more remote and mysterious parts of the countryside. Many mountains, rivers, and lakes in Japan are named after the dragons that just might, once, have lived there.

Japanese dragons are similar in appearance to the dragons of China. They are called tatsu or ryu and have long scaly bodies, four legs, whiskers, and three claws on their toes, but unlike Chinese dragons they also have a row of spines down their backs. These magical creatures control water, including rivers, and have power over the weather. They are thought to live in lakes, rivers, and springs and are associated with the Japanese emperor.

There are four Japanese dragon kings: Sui-Riu is the rain dragon who brings rain to the islands of Japan; Han-Riu is striped with nine different colors and is 12 meters (40 ft) long; Ri-Riu is a far-sighted dragon; and Ka-Riu is a small, red dragon, only 2 meters (6.5 ft) long.

The special dragon of good luck is Fuku-Riu, but to see any dragon was regarded as a lucky omen. The oldest and wisest of Japan's dragons can grow wings and become dragon birds or hai-riyo. Japanese dragons can also turn themselves into humans at will. They are generally friendly and gentle towards people, but not in every case, as the legend of Kyoto's dragon demonstrates.

KYOTO'S DRAGONS

There was once a time when the city of Kyoto was troubled by a white dragon that lived in a nearby lake. Every fifty years the dragon would transform into a magnificent yellow bird, an o-gon-cho, and fly from the lake with a terrible howling, which sounded like the cries of a wolf. The people of Kyoto dreaded this sound, as they knew it foretold the coming of a great famine. There were apparently several sightings of an o-gon-cho in April 1834, and sure enough, shortly afterwards there was widespread famine in the area.

Legend blames Japan's numerous, violent earthquakes and the fiercest of its storms on epic battles between the dragon and its arch-enemy, the tiger.

Kyoto is also protected by a dragon. On the eastern side of the city lies the Kiyomizu Temple of Seiryuu, the Azure Dragon. A statue of Seiryuu stands at the entrance. It is said to come to life and drink from a fountain at night.

Above Although Japanese dragons may look fearsome, they are usually benevolent and wise, putting their great powers over wind, weather, and water to good use.

Dragons' eggs

The eggs of Japanese dragons were thought to start life at the bottom of the ocean, where they would lie for 1,000 years. They would then rest in the mountains for a further 1,000 years and finally, for another 1,000 years, in a human village. At this stage they would look like beautiful, brightly colored stones, each with a tiny snake asleep within it. Attracted by the beautiful colors, people would pick up the stones and keep them in their houses. But anyone tempted to keep such a stone should beware. At the end of the three thousand years the stone would split and the tiny snake emerge. It would then grow alarmingly quickly and within just a few seconds smash its way through the roof amid a great storm of thunder and lighting, until it took on the form of a huge and magnificent dragon.

Right Japanese dragons' eggs spend a thousand years at the bottom of the ocean after they are first laid.

GREEK DRAGONS

Ancient Greek myths are full of tales of monsters—none more terrifying than the many-headed dragons that heroes like Hercules found themselves battling with. Here are three of the well-known tales about Greek dragons.

HERCULES AND THE DRAGONS

Hydra, a many-headed dragon with poisonous blood, lived in the swamp of Lerna, emerging every so often in search of cattle to eat. For the second of his twelve labors, Hercules was ordered to kill this beast. First, he drove the Hydra out if its swampy home and into the open by shooting fire-tipped arrows into its lair. He smote off head after head, but as each head was chopped off, two new heads would grow in its place. Eventually he defeated the beast with the help of his nephew, who seared the severed necks with fire the instant Hercules cut them, so that the heads could not grow back. The final head was immortal, so Hercules crushed it into the ground and covered it with a huge boulder.

Hercules also battled the dreadful Ladon in the garden of the Hesperides—the orchard of the goddess Hera and the beautiful home of three nymphs (the Hesperides). At the center of the garden stood a tree that bore golden apples. Twined around the tree, guarding the apples, was the hundred-headed serpent-dragon Ladon, who spoke in many different voices and never slept. For the eleventh of his labors, Hercules was told to steal the golden apples from the tree in the garden. Hercules made his way to the garden, crept up on the dragon, and shot it so accurately with an arrow that the creature died instantly. He stole the apples and fled. The goddess Hera put the slain dragon into the heavens as the star constellation Draco.

WHO WAS HERCULES?

Hercules (or Herakles) was the son of the god Zeus and Alcmene, a mortal woman. Zeus' wife, Hera, hated Hercules and tried to kill him or make difficulties for him whenever she could. Despite this, Hercules grew up brave and very strong. His famous twelve labors, each seemingly impossible, were tasks set by King Eurystheus, under orders from Hera. The second was to slay the terrible Hydra and the eleventh was to steal golden apples from under the noses of the dragon Ladon. In the end Hercules successfully completed all twelve of his labors. After a long and adventurous life, the hero finally died after putting on a poisoned shirt (see page 83).

Above *Immensely brave and strong, Hercules was arguably the greatest of the Greek heroes. Over the centuries, his legendary adventures have inspired countless artworks, such as this ancient statue, which stands in a museum in Naples, Italy.*

JASON AND THE GOLDEN FLEECE

Jason was prince of a land called Iolcus. He should rightfully have been king, but his wicked uncle had taken the throne in his place. To claim back his kingdom Jason was sent on a quest to bring back the fabled golden fleece that was kept in the far city of Colchis. The fleece was owned by King Aeetes and guarded by a dragon that never slept. Jason gathered a group of heroes, including Hercules and Theseus, and set sail in a ship called the Argo. After many adventures the Argonauts finally arrived at Colchis. King Aeetes agreed to give Jason the fleece, but only if he passed a terrifying test: first, he was to plough a field, using fire-breathing bulls to pull the plough; then he was to plant the field with dragon's teeth; these teeth would then grow into an army, which he must defeat. This task would have been impossible if it weren't for the help of the king's daughter, Medea, who had fallen in love with Jason. Medea was a sorceress. She protected Jason from the bulls' flames and instructed him to throw a rock into the midst of the dragon's teeth army. This he did, and the soldiers began fighting each other rather than him. Despite Jason's success, Aeetes still wouldn't give him the fleece, so Medea helped Jason again by bewitching the dragon so that he could steal it. Jason returned to Iolcus victorious and was crowned king at last.

THE WINNING OF THE GOLDEN FLEECE

Above Jason stole the golden fleece while Medea put the dragon to sleep with a magic charm.

Left Hercules battles the snaky heads of the dragon Hydra. All Greek dragons were many headed. Hercules is wearing the skin of the Nemean lion, which he slew in the first of his twelve labors.

DRAGON SLAYERS

Giant, scaly, winged, and fire-breathing, with vicious teeth and talons and perhaps spitting poison too—dragons must surely be the most terrifying of adversaries. There are many legends across the world of good overcoming evil when brave heroes slay dragons. Here are some examples.

SAINT GEORGE AND THE DRAGON

When a terrible dragon made its nest beside a spring in Cappadocia (in modern day Turkey) the local people were presented with a terrible problem. The spring was their only source of water, but to reach it, they had to get past the dragon. At first they managed to lure it away by offering it sheep to eat, but eventually the supply of sheep ran out. Unfortunately for the young girls of the area, the only solution seemed to be to offer them to the dragon instead of the sheep. Girls were selected for this terrible sacrifice by drawing lots, until one day, it was the king's

SUSA-NO-O AND YAMATA-NO-OROCHI

Susa-no-o, *Japanese god of storms, was wandering the Earth when he came across an elderly couple weeping over a beautiful young girl. They were her parents, and they were weeping because Yamata-no-orochi, a terrible eight-headed dragon, had devoured her seven sisters and would soon return for her, the eighth. The couple promised he could marry the girl if he slew the dragon, so Susa-no-o came up with a clever plan. He told the parents to make eight large tubs of sake (rice wine) and then he waited. Finally, the monster came for the girl. It was a terrifying sight—the length of eight hills, with trees growing along its back and eight spiked tails. When it saw the sake, it sank each head into a tub and greedily drank down all the wine. Before long, all eight heads were hopelessly drunk and fell asleep. Susa-no-o cut the stupefied dragon to pieces.*

Right *In this Japanese legend, Susa-no-o slays the terrible dragon and gets the girl.*

daughter herself who drew the fatal lot. The king begged for her to be spared, but the people insisted she must take her turn. Luckily for her, as she stood waiting for the awful creature to devour her, George, a brave Roman soldier passing through the country, came across the unhappy scene. He sprang into action. Protecting himself against the dragon by using the sign of the Christian cross, he took his lance and slew the great beast—saving the princess. The grateful people of Cappadocia immediately converted from their pagan religion to Christianity.

Above *Saint George was born near Jerusalem and is the patron saint of England, Ethiopia, Georgia, Greece, Palestine, Portugal, and Russia.*

SIGURD AND THE DRAGON

In Scandanavian mythology there is a story about a dwarf king called Hreidmar who had three sons: Fafnir, Otr, and Regin. One day, Otr was killed by the god Loki, and in recompense the god gave the dwarf king a great fortune in gold. The king's remaining sons wanted the gold for themselves and eventually killed their father for it. Fafnir, however, decided he didn't want to share the treasure with his brother. He stole it and fled to another land. Here he transformed into a terrible, wingless dragon so he could better guard his hoard.

In time, Regin became stepfather to a boy called Sigurd. When Sigurd grew up, Regin ordered him to find Fafnir and retrieve the gold. When Sigurd found the dragon, he dug a trench along a path the monster regularly used. He hid in this trench, and as the dragon stepped over him he thrust his sword into the beast's belly and killed him. He was drenched in the dragon's blood, which miraculously gave him the power to understand all languages, including those of animals. He was warned by a bird that his stepfather Regin intended to kill him. Sigurd slew Regin before he could act, keeping all of the gold for himself. But the fortune brought him no happiness.

FOUR-LEGGED FIENDS

Beasts patched together from several different creatures or familiar animal friends turned bad: this collection of four-legged fiends horrify and fascinate in equal measure. From the terrifying three-headed Cerberus and crocodile-headed Ammut—both denizens of the underworld—to the vampire cat of Japan and the cunning Greek sphinx, these creatures guard their territories jealously. It's a brave person who dares to take them on. A few heroes have succeeded in conquering these monsters, however; some by force, others by cunning, and all with a good deal of courage.

1 Greece
Cerberus, the riddle-telling sphinx; Chimera

2 Egypt
Heart-devouring Ammut, Anubis, sphinxes

3 Japan
Vampire cats, kitsune, vampire foxes

4 England
Questing Beast of Arthurian legend, flying Gabriel Hounds, Barguest, Black Shuck, the mysterious Beast of Dartmoor

5 Wales
Cwm Annwyn hounds

6 Scotland
The doom-laden Cu Sith

7 Middle East
Griffins, manticore

8 India
Treasure-guarding griffins, manticore

9 Europe
The half-horse, half-griffin hippogriffs, griffins

10 Germany
Wild Hunt

11 Scandanavia
Woden's hunt

12 China
Hu-hsein

13 Ethiopia
Manticore

14 Canada
Waheela

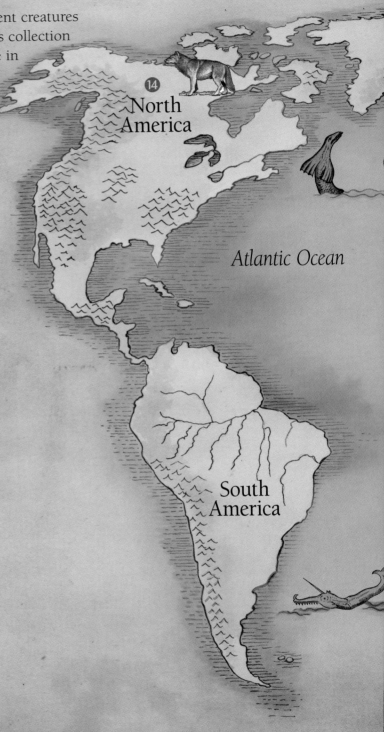

North America

Atlantic Ocean

South America

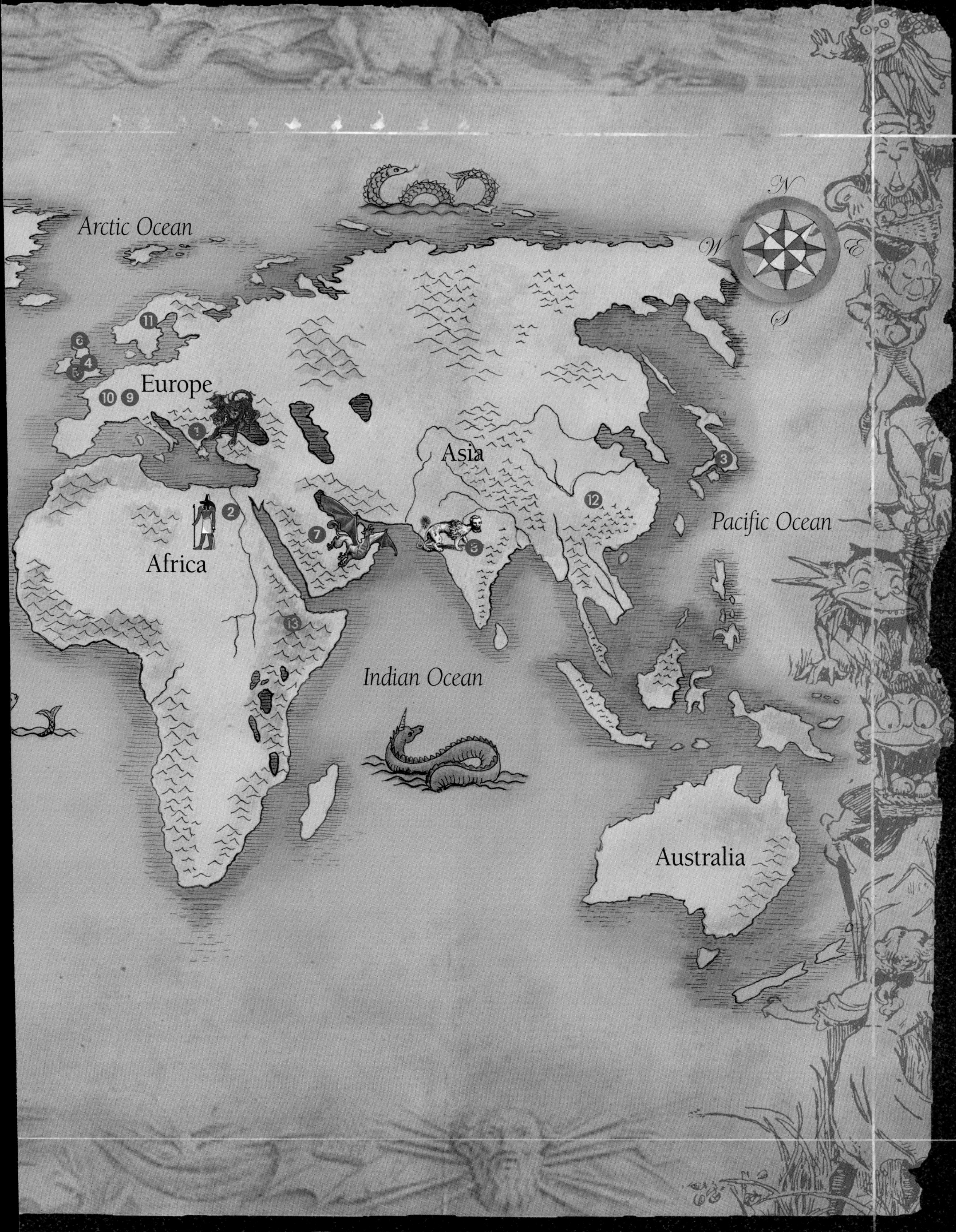

N
W
E
S
Arctic Ocean
Europe
Asia
Africa
Pacific Ocean
Indian Ocean
Australia
1
2
3
4
5
6
7
8
9
10
11
12
13

Vampire Cats

Some of the most frightening moments happen when normal or familiar things turn bad. Look again at that sweet bundle of fur that shares your house and purrs in front of your hearth. Does an evil vampire heart lurk within? This Japanese legend tells of just such an animal.

Fantastical fact

The Ainu people of Japan believe that if a person kills a cat, it will avenge itself by bewitching them: they are condemned to waste away and die, all the while behaving like a cat and miaowing pitifully. This bizarre death can only be prevented if the person eats some part of the cat they have killed.

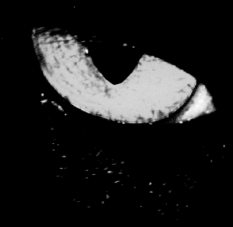

The vampire cat of Nabeshima

There once was a prince who was in love with a beautiful maiden. One day when they had been out walking they were followed home by a large cat. That night, at midnight, the cat crept into the girl's bedroom, leapt upon her neck, and bit her to death. It dragged her body into the garden, dug a hole, and buried her bloody corpse. Then it assumed the shape of the girl, and no one, not even the prince, was any the wiser. But from that day onwards, the prince's strength began to ebb away. He became pale and listless, and was troubled in his sleep by terrifying dreams. His doctors were at a loss as to what was wrong, for little did they realize that each night, the cat-girl visited the prince and drained the life force from him.

The people of the prince's court became concerned about his dreams, and a battalion of soldiers was ordered to keep watch over him at night, but each evening at ten o'clock, the soldiers were seized by an irresistible drowsiness and fell asleep. Then one day a loyal and gentle soldier called Itô Sôda came to the palace and begged to be allowed to keep guard one night. The prince's advisers agreed. They warned him about the strange drowsiness that had overcome the other soldiers. So Itô Sôda went prepared: when ten o'clock came and he felt the drowsiness creep over him, he stuck a small knife into his thigh, twisting it each time he

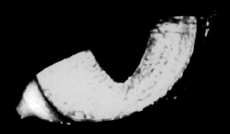

felt sleepy. The pain kept him awake, and at midnight he saw the girl creep silently into the room. As she approached the prince, she saw that Itô Sôda was still awake and questioned him. He explained what he had done, and she left, unable to perform her nightly transformation. This happened again the next night. On the third night, the girl didn't come at all, and the other soldiers stayed awake. By this time the prince, having avoided the horrors of the cat's visits for several nights, had slept well and was looking much better. Itô Sôda was convinced by this that the girl was the source of the trouble. He decided to go to her room and confront her. Under attack, the girl fought back fiercely, but realizing she could not win, she turned back into a cat, clawed her way up the wall, out onto the roof, and away. She escaped into the mountains and there she stayed, making much trouble and mischief for the local people. Finally, the prince ordered a massive hunt for her and she was found and killed. As for Itô Sôda—he was richly rewarded for his loyalty and cleverness.

Left The unearthly shine of cats' eyes when caught in the light, and their unnerving, unblinking stare, may well have fuelled stories about them having supernatural, and sometimes evil, powers.

VAMPIRE FOXES

The hu-hsien of China are evil, shape-shifting fox spirits that can take on human form. They drain the life out of their human lovers to increase their own strength. But they cannot resist wine, and if they get drunk, they lose their human appearance, revealing their true and terrible nature. Japanese myths also feature fox spirits, called kitsune, that take human form. Some feed on their lovers like the hu-hsien, but most kitsune are magical, mischievous, long-lived, and wise.

Right In one of the stories about kitsune, a fox-woman called Kuzunoha marries a man who saves her from hunters. Only her shadow gives away her true identity.

THE GRIFFIN

With the golden-furred body of a lion—the king of the beasts—and the proud head, wings, and talons of an eagle—the king of the birds—the griffin is the most majestic of all mythological beasts. It is a symbol of strength and protection and was once the guardian of priceless hoards of gold in the kingdoms of ancient Arabia and India.

Although it is majestic, the griffin is also a powerful and sometimes terrifying creature. To the ancient Egyptians and Persians, griffins represented dark or evil powers. In some stories they were vicious and greedy, attacking anything that came near them. In India, ancient Arabia, and ancient Greece, their great fierceness was put to good use in their role as guardians of treasure or protectors of sacred places and important people. There is a legend about Alexander the Great—the Greek conquering hero who lived over 2,000 years ago—in which he tames eight griffins, harnessing them to a chariot and flying to the heavens. In medieval times, griffins became popular beasts to feature on coats of arms as they represented desirable qualities, such as strength and watchfulness.

Above *The strong, loyal, and ever-watchful griffin was a popular figure on coats of arms.*

SYMBOL OF EMPIRE

In Roman mythology griffins pulled the chariot of Nemesis, the goddess of justice, who flew around the world helping the good and punishing the wicked by running over them with her chariot wheels. This link with law and justice prompted the Romans to take the griffin as the symbol of their empire, representing the principles of government they carried with them as the empire spread across the known world. The Romans also used images of griffins on graves, as it was believed they would protect the dead and guide their souls safely to the afterlife.

GRIFFINS AND HARRY POTTER

In the Harry Potter books, Gryffindor is the name of the school house that Harry and his friends belong to. Although its symbol is a lion rather than a griffin, the qualities of strength, courage, and vigilance that the griffin embodies are very much those prized by the house and its founder, Godric Gryffindor.

Hippogriffs, which are a strange combination of the front part of a griffin and the back part of a horse, also appear in the Harry Potter books. These weird creatures were invented by an Italian poet Ludovico Ariosto 500 years ago. There was a saying at the time that described an impossible task as being "like trying to cross griffins with horses," because griffins and horses were said to be mortal enemies. Ariosto thought it would be amusing to imagine what the offspring of a griffin and a horse would look like and came up with the hippogriff (*hippo* means "horse" in Latin).

Fantastical fact

In medieval times, griffins' claws were said to be able to detect poison and were highly prized. In fact, supposed griffin claws from that time have turned out to be ibex horns (an ibex is a type of goat).

QUESTING BEAST

Lions were a popular choice in the make-up of fantastical animals. There were griffins, the Chimera, manticores, sphinxes, and, perhaps strangest of all, the medieval Questing Beast, which appears in the English legends of King Arthur. This peculiar creature, with a serpent's head, a leopard's body, a lion's hindquarters, and the hooves of a deer, was continually running to seek water with which to slake its unquenchable thirst. Unfortunately, it poisoned any water it drank from. As the beast ran, its belly made a sound like a pack of hounds baying when looking—or questing—for their quarry.

Right *King Arthur wakes from a dream and sees the Questing Beast drinking next to him.*

Left *Part eagle, part lion—a giant and powerful griffin takes to the skies.*

ARTHVR·AND·THE·QUESTING·BEAST

SPHINX

Either the gentle symbol of the rising sun or a bloodthirsty monster, the sphinx has two distinctly different characters depending on whether it is Egyptian or Greek. What the two types do have in common, however, is that they both have the body of a lion but the head of another creature.

The ancient Egyptians believed that their gods and pharaohs had close links with particular animals. One of the ways they demonstrated these beliefs was by making figures that were part-man and part-animal. They called such figures *shesep-ankh*, which means "living statue." This eventually became "sphinx." Sphinxes had lions' bodies and the heads of either rams, hawks, or people. They were the guardians of tombs, sacred roads, and pyramids and represented the rising sun.

EGYPTIAN SPHINX

The most famous of all sphinxes is the huge statue in the desert beside the great pyramids at Giza, which has the body of a lion and the head of a pharaoh. The monument is over 70 meters (230 ft) long and was carved out of the rock more than 4500 years ago. About 1,000 years after it was fashioned, it had become almost completely covered by the shifting desert sands, with only its head still visible. It is said that around this time a young prince fell asleep under its shadow. The sphinx appeared to him in a dream and told him that if he cleared away the sand, he would become pharaoh. The dream came true—the prince shifted the sand from around the statue and became Pharaoh Tuthmosis IV.

THE RIDDLE OF THE GREEK SPHINX

Moving in or out of the city of Thebes, in ancient Greece, was a treacherous business. Travelers had to get past the cunning sphinx, a monstrous creature with the head and chest of a woman, the body of a lion, the wings of an eagle, and the tail of a serpent. She lay in wait on the cliffs that loomed over the only pass into the city, waiting to challenge people with a riddle. If they failed to solve it, this hideous monster would strangle and devour them without a second's hesitation. The riddle the sphinx asked was this: "What walks on four legs in the morning, two legs at noon, and three legs in the evening and is weakest when it walks on the most?" No one had ever managed to solve it—all had been eaten.

One day a man called Oedipus approached her. He had a flash of inspiration and said that the answer was a man, for he crawls on all fours as a baby, walks on two legs as a man, and leans on a stick to help him in old age. He is the weakest when he is a baby. Incandescent with rage that someone had at last solved her puzzle, the sphinx screamed and threw herself off the cliff, smashing into thousands of tiny pieces on the rocks below. Not surprisingly, the grateful people of Thebes then made Oedipus their king.

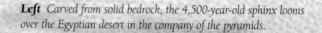

***Above** The bloodthirsty manticore is said to have an insatiable appetite for human flesh.*

THE MANTICORE

At first glance, the manticore of Persia (modern-day Iran), India, and Ethiopia appears very much like the Egyptian sphinx, having the body of a red lion and a human head. But there the similarity ends. Unlike the gentle Egyptian sphinx, the manticore is a terrifying and bloodthirsty monster. In its mouth are three rows of sharp teeth, and it uses a strangely alluring trumpeting call to draw its victims near. The beast may be horned, winged, or both and has the tail of a scorpion or dragon, with poisonous spines which it can shoot out like darts. This vicious animal—its name means "man eater"—pursues its quarry with relentless speed then paralyzes its victims with poison from its tail spines. It will completely devour its unfortunate prey: bones, clothing, possessions, and all.

105

AMMUT

Devourer, Eater of Hearts, Bone Eater, and Greatness of Death, the ancient Egyptian figure of Ammut had many names, each more horrifying than the next. But this is fitting when you consider Ammut's task: to sit at the judgement of the dead and eat the unworthy hearts of the wicked!

Above *Ammut waits eagerly as Anubis weighs the heart of a traveler to the Underworld, ready to devour it if it fails the test.*

The ancient Egyptians believed that when a person died, their *ka*, or life-force, traveled to the Underworld, where it was led to a pair of scales. Their heart was weighed against the feather of truth by Anubis, the god of embalming. The result was recorded by Thoth, the god of wisdom and writing. If the heart was lighter than the feather, the ka would pass on to the afterlife. If it was heavier, Ammut, denizen of the Underworld, sat ready and waiting to devour it—the soul was then doomed to be restless forever. Ammut was not a god but more like a demon. She was not worshiped, but she was certainly

ANUBIS

Anubis was the gatekeeper of the underworld, guardian of tombs, and god of embalming. He is shown as having the head of a jackal or a dog. Jackals were associated with death, because they were scavengers and likely to dig up dead bodies. Anubis is jet black, the same color that dead bodies turn when they have been embalmed. No one knows for sure where the name Anubis comes from, but some think it might be an ancient Egyptian word that means to putrefy or rot. Others think it could mean "royal child" as Anubis was the son of Osiris, king of the Underworld. Anubis had the vitally important job of protecting the dead on their journey to the weighing of the heart ceremony and on to the afterlife. Professional embalmers often wore Anubis masks while they went about their grisly business of turning dead bodies into mummies.

Right *Jackal-headed Anubis was once the lord of the afterlife, until the god Osiris took over. Afterwards he remained the god of embalming and guardian of the dead.*

feared and very scary to look at, with the head of a crocodile or dog, the upper body of a lion or leopard, and the rear end of a hippopotamus. Some believed that Ammut stood by a lake of fire, casting the unworthy hearts into the lake rather than eating them; others feared that she ate the whole person rather than just the heart, the body then dissolving in her stomach.

PROTECTIVE MEASURES

Fortunately for some, even if you had not led a perfect life, you could protect yourself from Ammut if you were rich and clever enough to have sacred amulets, such as scarabs, folded in your wrappings when your body was embalmed and mummified. These would prevent Anubis and Ammut from discovering any of your guilty secrets, which might otherwise have made your heart too heavy to pass the ultimate test.

Right *Many Egyptian gods and goddesses were shown with the heads of beasts and birds as symbols of their roles and abilities. This is Thoth, god of wisdom, with the head of an ibis.*

CERBERUS

You might think that dying was bad enough, but if you were facing death in ancient Greece, that was just the start of your troubles. Before your soul could be at rest, it had to first cross the River Acheron with the sinister ferryman, Charon; then it must face the terrifying, three-headed monster Cerberus at the entrance to the Underworld.

CERBERUS AND HERCULES

Capturing Cerberus and bringing him back alive was the twelfth and final labor given to Hercules by King Eurystheus (see page 94). By now, Hercules was sick and tired of these labors. He stormed down to the Underworld, so frightening Charon that the ferryman agreed to take him across the River Acheron to Hades, even though he was not dead. Hercules then marched up to Hades and demanded that he let him borrow his dog. Hades agreed, but only on the condition that Hercules didn't use any weapons against Cerberus.

This arrangement suited the super-strong Hercules just fine. He simply gripped the monstrous dog by the neck and wrestled it to the ground. Then he flung it over his shoulders and carted it back to Eurystheus. The cowardly king had thought this last labor was truly impossible and was so surprised and terrified to see Hercules return with the three-headed hell-hound that he jumped into a large storage jar to hide! The mission completed, Hercules let Cerberus go, and he bounded off back to Hades.

Above *Hercules single-handedly dragged Cerberus from the Underworld.*

Hades, the land of the dead, was the gloomy place where all mortals' souls were doomed to end up. The role of Cerberus was to guard the entrance to Hades: he would devour any living being that tried to get in. He was also there to ensure that no dead souls could escape from the Underworld, which was ruled by Cerberus's master, the god of the dead (also called Hades). Terrifying to look upon, in some stories Cerberus had 50 or even 100 heads, but most tales describe him as having three—one like a lion's, one like a dog's, and the third like a wolf's—representing the past, present, and future. He was a huge beast, the size of bullock, and had a mane of writhing snakes and a serpent's tail.

Cerberus is not the only canine guardian of the dead. Myths from Central Asia, Siberia, India, and Scandinavia all feature terrifying, dog-like monsters that act as sentinels of the Underworld.

How to get past the Hound of Hell

Hercules is one of very few people who managed to get past Cerberus. Those who did used various methods. Here are some tactics to employ if you ever find yourself facing the Hound of Hell.

- Lull him to sleep with soothing music—this was what the Greek musician Orpheus did when he traveled to the Underworld to bring back his dead wife, Eurydice.
- Show him a little kindness—in one version of the Hercules story, the hero gently persuades the monster to go with him rather than wrestling him to the ground.
- Drug him—the god Hermes used this method. He put the giant dog to sleep by giving him magical water from the River Lethe to drink.
- Feed him—Roman hero Aeneas and renowned beauty Psyche both fed Cerberus honeycakes that sent him to sleep. If you try this, make sure you have a cake for each head!
- Wrestle him into submission—this is the least complicated approach, but keep in mind that you have to be as strong as Hercules to attempt something as dangerous as this!

Above right *The three heads of Cerberus represent past, present, and future.*

THE WAHEELA

In one of the most remote valleys of the world, part of the vast Northwest Territories of Canada, there has been a string of unexplained and gruesome deaths. The Nahinni Valley has become known as Headless Valley because several human bodies have been found there with one vital thing missing … their heads. Local people have no doubt that the creature responsible is the Waheela, a gigantic, wolf-like beast of Indian legend. Taller than a wolf, with a broad head, an almost bear-like bulk, and very long, white fur, this beast hunts alone and keeps to the remotest corners of the valley. But it defends its territory mercilessly if any unfortunate person stumbles across it. Some scientists think that if such an animal exists it could be a prehistoric species of wolf that has somehow survived until the present day. Native legends tell a different story, however: that the Waheela is an evil spirit with supernatural powers. Either way, the creature should be avoided at all costs!

Above *Fact or myth? The Waheela of Canada's Nahinni Valley is said to take the form of a giant and vicious white wolf.*

BLACK DOGS AND DEATH HOUNDS

Terrifying phantom dogs—from death-foretelling, black hounds with fiery eyes and sulfurous breath to flying, human-headed Gabriel Hounds of northern England—abound in the folk tales of Europe, particularly Britain. If you hear a blood-curdling howl on a deserted, night-time road, beware!

Above *In a scene from Arthur Conan Doyle's "The Hound of the Baskervilles," the terrifying black dog of the title is shot dead.*

Dogs have been the companions of humans for longer than any other animal. They are loyal and brave and have served humans in many ways. It is therefore particularly terrifying when such a familiar animal turns bad. Apparitions of huge and ghastly black dogs with eyes like fiery coals are known all across Britain, and tales about them have been told since Viking times, well over a thousand years ago. Barguest, Black Shuck, Gurt Dog, Devil's Dandy, Wisht Hound, and Gytrash are just a few examples. They are usually seen on dark, deserted roads and may track hapless travelers for miles, bringing misfortune or foretelling death or disaster. It is very unwise to approach such a black dog, as if they attack, their wounds can be terrible, failing to heal or leading to paralysis or even death.

PACK HUNTERS

Sometimes spectral hounds appear in packs—such as the Gabriel Hounds or Gabble Ratchets in northern England, the Wild Hunt in Germany, and the Woden's Hunt in Scandinavia. The Gabriel Hounds have human heads and fly in the air. If they hover over a house, then someone inside is soon going to die. In Wales, corpse dogs—the Cwm Annwyn hounds of fairyland—are usually invisible or appear as huge, white hounds with red eyes and ears. They howl horribly, prophesying death and seeking out corpses and the souls of the dead. They are led either by the devil or by a monstrous, black-faced huntsman, Gwyn ap Nudd.

Scotland has its own tradition of phantom hounds. Farmers in the Highlands are always very wary of any mysterious barking or howling drifting over the moors. This is likely to be the call of the Cu Sith, an enormous, green hound with a long, braided tail arched over its back. This cow-sized canine runs like lightning, bellowing after its prey. On hearing its terrifying howl, farmers who lived nearby would lock up their womenfolk for fear that the hound would abduct them and take them to a fairy mound to supply milk for hungry fairy children.

Beast of Dartmoor

Large, uninhabited areas, such as Dartmoor in southwest England, seem particularly likely to attract stories of mysterious and terrifying beasts. Sightings of large, predatory animals on Dartmoor have occurred for hundreds of years. These may have some basis in fact. Exotic animals, including lions and pumas, began to be brought into England from almost 400 years ago as part of "menageries"—private zoos for the very rich. Tales of phantom animals might stem from sightings of real animals that escaped from such menageries. There is plenty of room and plenty of free-roaming prey on Dartmoor (including sheep and ponies) for such an animal to survive virtually unseen for years.

Escaped exotic animals may also explain more recent sightings of the so-called "Beast of Dartmoor," said to be a giant, cat-like creature. In 1976, a change in the law meant that anyone who kept a dangerous animal had to be far more accountable than they had been in the past. A few irresponsible owners might have let their animals loose in the wild rather than face the strict new rules. If the beast does exist, it may well be one of these. It is also likely to be more than one animal. People have described creatures of different sizes and colors, some dog-like, some feline. Some have been positively identified as large dogs. In one case, the culprit was an escaped lion! Other sightings still remain mysterious.

Right *This photograph, taken in the southwest of England, is one of many perplexing snapshots of unidentified local "beasts."*

FABULOUS BIRDS

The immortal phoenix lives for centuries before being consumed by flames and then emerging reborn from its own ashes. This is one of the best known of all mythological birds. But there are others too: the awe inspiring Thunderbird of the native North Americans; the giant roc of the Arabian Nights stories; and the benevolent and beautiful simurgh of Persia (now Iran). Russian stories about winged and feathered creatures include the magnificent firebird, whose feathers burn like flames, and the beautiful but deadly winged sirin, who bewitch the unwary with their haunting songs.

❶ North America
Thunderbird, the bringer of storms; Raven, the trickster

❷ Russia
The sirin

❸ Wales
Bloduewedd—flower faced owl maiden

❹ Persia
Simurgh

❺ Middle East
The roc famously encountered by Sindbad, the immortal phoenix

❻ China
Fenghuang

❼ Madagascar
Aepyornis the real-life elephant bird

❽ India
Garuda the divine king of birds

❾ Greece
The beautiful but deadly sirens, the Stymphalian birds

❿ Japan
Ho-oo

Arctic Ocean

Europe

Africa

Asia

Indian Ocean

Pacific Ocean

Australia

THE PHOENIX

Famous for dying in flames before being reborn, the phoenix is the most dramatic of mythical birds. The classic phoenix legends are associated with ancient Arabia and Egypt, but a similar type of bird can be found in the stories of other cultures, including those of China and Japan.

The Arabian phoenix, according to tales passed down by ancient Greek and Roman writers, was the size of an eagle. Some say it had glowing red and golden feathers, while others describe it as having a purple body and a rich blue or azure tail, with a tuft of feathers on its head. Its song was sweet and tuneful. Living near a shady well in the wilds of Arabia, it would wake at daybreak and break into captivating song. The phoenix did not kill or harm anything for its food, but lived instead on droplets of morning dew that formed during the night.

REBORN IN FLAMES

There was only a single phoenix existing at any one time. But it lived a long life—some say 500 years, while others claim it survived for 1,461 or even 12,994 years. It was at the moment of its death that the bird's magical nature became obvious. As its life was coming to an end, it would build a nest from sweet-smelling twigs and spices such as cinnamon. Then, sitting in the nest, the bird set it on fire and was engulfed by the flames. Some say that the phoenix was consumed by the raging flames to rise again from the smoldering ashes. Another version says a worm emerges from the ashes, which turns into a tiny bird on the second day and a fully grown phoenix on the third. The tears of the phoenix were said to have the magical power to heal or even to temporarily protect a person from death.

Right   This is a traditional image of a phoenix rising again from the flames of its funeral pyre. The phoenix is often used as a symbol of rebuilding and rebirth.

Fantastical fact

In Russian folklore, the feathers of the beautiful and mystical firebird glow like gold, red, and orange flames. The feathers continue to glow even when removed, bringing light and hope to the hearts of men.

THE FENGHUANG AND HO-OO

The phoenix-like Chinese fenghuang had a snake's neck, a swallow's face, and a cock's beak. Its breast was that of a goose, and it had the back of a tortoise and the tail of a fish. Prized as an emblem of good luck, the fenghuang sang beautiful songs. The Japanese ho-oo was in fact two birds, the ho being the male, and the oo the female. It resembled the fenghuang in looks. The appearance of the ho-oo was believed to mark the birth of a good ruler.

Right *In this 100-year-old embroidery, a gorgeously colored Chinese phoenix sits resplendent in a tree surrounded by lesser birds.*

115

THE THUNDERBIRD

Native American people may have once looked up at the skies with fear during thunderstorms. Their legends tell that every clap of thunder is the wingbeat of a massive flying terror—the Thunderbird. Every lightning flash is a blink of the Thunderbird's giant eyes.

THUNDERBIRD AND THE WHALE

Once there was a monstrous whale that attacked and killed others of its own kind until there were no more whales for people to hunt. From his home high in the mountains, Thunderbird saw what was happening and became angry. As long as two war canoes, with a giant beak and eyes like glowing coals, Thunderbird soared from his high mountain. He plunged into the sea, and grabbed the whale with his vast claws. There was a huge battle between the whale and Thunderbird and a great shaking, jumping up, and trembling of the earth and a rolling up of the great waters. The ocean fell and then rose again, canoes were flung ashore, and many people were killed in the mayhem. Finally, Thunderbird managed to drag the whale out of the ocean and into the air. When he had flown high enough he dropped the whale, and the battle continued on the ground until finally Thunderbird won, and the people could hunt whales once more.

Flying high above the earth, the Thunderbird pulled clouds together with its giant wings, creating storms and rain as it went. As well as flashing sheet lightning from its eyes, it carried glowing snakes in its claws that made lightning bolts. Thunderbird had feathers of shimmering colors and rows of sharp teeth in its giant beak. The power of the Thunderbird was the greatest power in the whole universe—the power of hot and cold clashing above the clouds.

Some people believed that there were many Thunderbirds. These beings, they thought, could shape-shift into human form by shrugging off their feathers and opening their beaks to reveal human faces inside. In this form they might marry into human tribes. Although Thunderbird was frightening, he was also a protector and friend to humans, as the story of Thunderbird and the whale shows.

Fantastical fact

In the story of the fight between the whale and Thunderbird, the earth shakes and the ocean rolls away and floods back again. This refers to the effects of real-life earthquakes and tsunamis (giant ocean waves).

Left *A stern image of Thunderbird tops this totem pole, carved by the native people of Vancouver, Canada. Totem poles are usually created to record stories, events, and family relationships.*

RAVEN

In many stories from North America Raven is the creator of the world. Before the time of people Raven lived in the spirit world, but he got bored so he flew away from there, carrying a stone in his beak. After a while he became tired of carrying the stone and dropped it into the ocean, where it grew and grew until it formed the world. Another story tells how Raven found a clam and opened it to discover creatures inside. They were timid and frightened, but he coaxed them out and into the world. These were the first men. But Raven soon got bored with the creatures and was about to put them back in the shell when he decided to look for female humans instead. He eventually found some trapped inside a different type of shell and was greatly amused by watching the men and women meet and interact. From that day on, Raven was very protective of humans.

Above right *Raven, who features in creation stories from North America, was a great trickster.*

THE ROC

Large enough to scoop up a fully grown elephant in its gigantic claws, the roc, or rukh, was a fantastic bird of Arabian legend. It was terrifying to look at—resembling a colossal eagle or vulture with horns. As well as eating elephants, the roc was said to have a taste for human flesh.

"For all the world like an eagle, but one indeed of enormous size; and so strong that it will seize an elephant in its talons and carry him high into the air and drop him so that he is smashed to pieces; having so killed him, the bird swoops down on him and eats him at leisure." These are the words of the Italian adventurer Marco Polo describing a roc 700 years ago. He added that the roc was usually white and had a wingspan of

15 meters (50 ft) and feathers 7 meters (23 ft) long. When it flew, the beating of its wings caused high winds, and its flight created lightning. In other stories rocs were attracted to human flesh and would pick dead bodies off battlefields. Perhaps the best-known encounters with the roc were those of Sindbad in the Arabian Nights stories.

Right *The majestic roc was able to carry enormous creatures in its massive talons, such as this elephant and rhinoceros.*

SINDBAD AND THE ROC

On his second voyage of adventure, Sindbad found himself deserted by his shipmates on a beautiful island. As there was no obvious way to escape, he decided to explore his island prison and saw in the distance a huge white dome. He approached it with caution and walked all round it but could find no way in. Suddenly, the sky darkened, and a huge shape came flying towards him. He realized the shape was a roc, a gigantic and monstrous bird, and the dome was, in fact, its egg. The bird came to rest on the egg, settled its wings around it, and fell asleep. Sindbad saw his chance to escape. He took his turban off his head and unwound the long length of material. He used it to tie himself to the sleeping bird's giant foot and waited until morning. Sure enough, when dawn broke the great bird lifted off into the air, completely unaware that Sindbad was lashed to its claws. They flew so high that a terrified Sindbad thought they must surely have reached the heavens. When the bird came down to land, Sindbad hurriedly undid the turban and stole away before the bird noticed him.

On his fifth voyage Sindbad came across the rocs again. In this story Sindbad's shipmates destroy a roc egg, and its angry parents wreck their ship by dropping rocks on it.

Above *Despite Sindbad's warnings, his foolhardy shipmates destroyed a roc egg, inviting the wrath of its parents.*

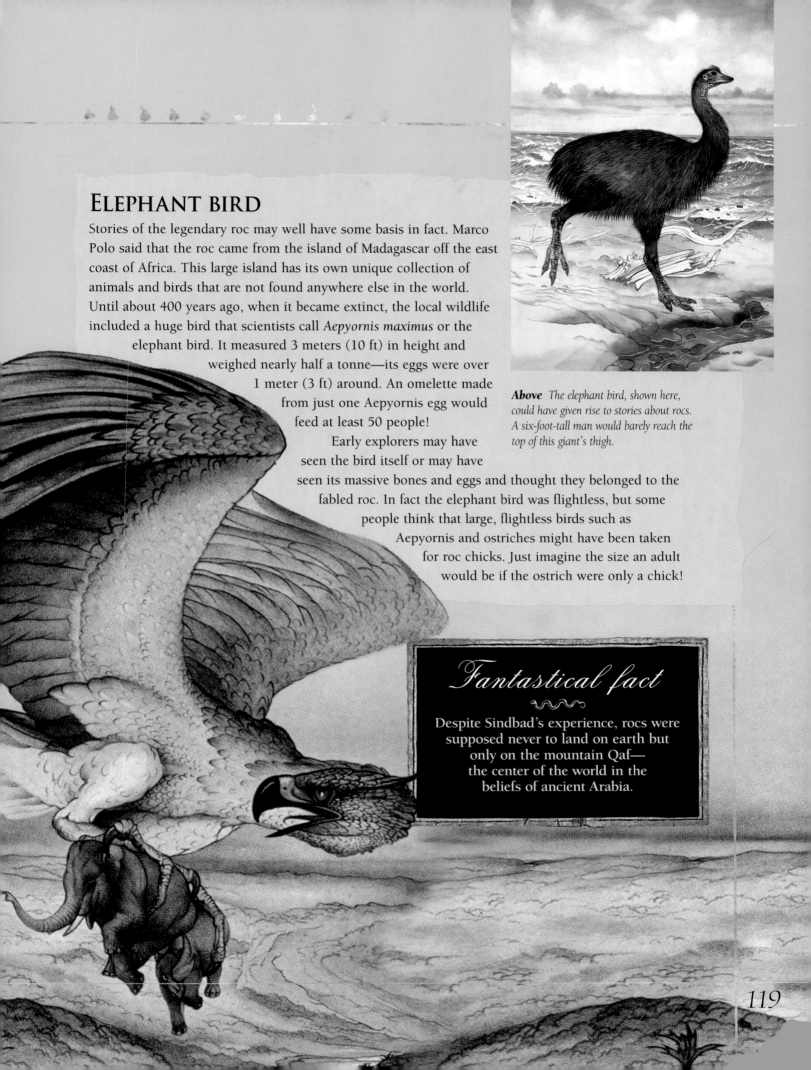

ELEPHANT BIRD

Stories of the legendary roc may well have some basis in fact. Marco Polo said that the roc came from the island of Madagascar off the east coast of Africa. This large island has its own unique collection of animals and birds that are not found anywhere else in the world. Until about 400 years ago, when it became extinct, the local wildlife included a huge bird that scientists call *Aepyornis maximus* or the elephant bird. It measured 3 meters (10 ft) in height and weighed nearly half a tonne—its eggs were over 1 meter (3 ft) around. An omelette made from just one Aepyornis egg would feed at least 50 people!

Early explorers may have seen the bird itself or may have seen its massive bones and eggs and thought they belonged to the fabled roc. In fact the elephant bird was flightless, but some people think that large, flightless birds such as Aepyornis and ostriches might have been taken for roc chicks. Just imagine the size an adult would be if the ostrich were only a chick!

Above *The elephant bird, shown here, could have given rise to stories about rocs. A six-foot-tall man would barely reach the top of this giant's thigh.*

Fantastical fact

Despite Sindbad's experience, rocs were supposed never to land on earth but only on the mountain Qaf— the center of the world in the beliefs of ancient Arabia.

119

THE SIMURGH

Part bird, part lion, and part dog, the Simurgh of ancient Persia was certainly mixed up! Like the roc it was also a giant of the skies—so big it could carry a whale in its giant claws. But despite its great size and frightening appearance the Simurgh was a wise and good creature.

The Simurgh was certainly a strange beast to look at—it had the head of a dog, the body of a lion, and the wings and tail of a peacock. Persian (Iranian) legends say the simurgh lived in the Tree of Life, a magical tree whose seeds were supposed to cure every disease. The Simurgh shook the tree and scattered the seeds all over the world so that people everywhere would have healing plants. The touch of a Simurgh feather was also said to have the power to cure the sick.

The Simurgh was very old and wise. It had lived so long that it had seen the destruction of the world three times over. Some stories say it was consumed by fire every 1,700 years and then reborn again, in much the same way as the phoenix.

According to one old Persian myth, the Simurgh once found a baby abandoned in the rocky wasteland near where it lived.

She took pity on the child, a boy called Zal, and looked after him for many years, bringing him up and teaching him the ways of the world. When at last the time came for Zal to make his own way in life, the simurgh gave him one of her golden breast feathers and told him to cast it in the fire if he ever needed her help. Zal left the simurgh with a heavy heart, but he went back into the world, inherited a kingdom, which he ruled wisely, and married a beautiful girl. When his wife started giving birth to their first child, Zal realised the baby was too big and that both mother and child were in grave danger. He cast the simurgh feather into the fire. The great bird appeared instantly and safely delivered the child, who was named Rustam and grew up to be a great Persian hero.

Right *Here, the Simurgh finds abandoned baby Zal and carries him to her nest. The illustration is from a 16th-century version of the* Shahnameh, *an epic book of Persian (Iranian) myths.*

GARUDA

Garuda is a divine man-bird—king of the birds in the Hindu myths of India. He, along with the eight elephants that support the universe, was born from a cosmic egg at the beginning of the world. He is a huge and fantastical creature with the body of a man but the wings and beak of an eagle. Garuda shines brighter than the sun and can easily fly across the universe. He was born hating all evil things and flew round the world devouring anything he came across that was bad or wicked. Like the Simurgh, he is the mortal enemy of snakes. Garuda is often ridden by the great Hindu god Vishnu and his female companion, Lakshmi.

Above *The god Vishnu is said to ride on the back of Garuda, the divine man-bird.*

FEATHERED FIENDS

At first you can hardly hear anything, just a faint but beautiful sound carried on the wind. It's so haunting and lovely that you strain to hear more. The singing grows louder and more intense until it blocks out everything else in your mind. It is beautiful and terrible at the same time, but you cannot resist it. You cannot escape the song of the siren ….

How to escape a siren song

* Plug your ears so you cannot hear their enchanted singing.

* Ask someone to restrain you so you cannot follow their song.

* Play music yourself that is even more beautiful than their singing—the lyre player Orpheus did this effectively in the Greek story of Jason and the Argonauts.

* Make loud noises to drown out their song. In Russia, people use canon fire and bells to cover the songs of sirin.

In the myths of the ancient Greeks the sirens were beautiful maidens with human heads but the bodies, wings, and legs of birds, whose enchanted singing lured ships to their doom on the sharp, treacherous rocks surrounding their island home. The terrible sirens would then devour the unfortunate, shipwrecked sailors, tearing them to pieces with their hooked talons. They made their nests amongst the bleached bones of their victims.

One of the most famous tales of the sirens involves Odysseus, the hero of the Trojan War, who had to sail past their island on his long voyage home. Odysseus managed

Below *Lashed firmly to the mast of his ship, Odysseus was saved from the unearthly song of the sirens.*

to escape their deadly song by telling his crew to stop up their ears with wax, blocking out the fateful singing. But he himself was burning with curiosity to hear the sirens' song, so he ordered his men to lash him to the mast, preventing him from leaping into the water in an attempt to reach the malicious maidens. This the crew did and, though he struggled wildly to escape when he heard the singing, the ropes held and Odysseus survived unscathed.

THE SIRIN

Russian folklore features a similar creature, the sirin, which had the head and face of a beautiful maiden and the body of a bird, usually an owl. If you were a saint, you had nothing to fear from sirin, who would sing you beautiful songs about the joys of eternal life. Mere mortals, however, had much more to worry about. If they heard the sirin's song they would forget everything and follow the sirin blindly until they eventually died of starvation and exhaustion.

Above The beautiful but deadly song of the Russian sirin makes ordinary mortals forget everything and abandon their loved ones.

Fantastical fact

Although they had wings, the sirens couldn't fly. Their flight feathers were removed as a punishment when they lost a music contest with the Muses—goddesses of the arts.

BLODEUWEDD

I n this legend from Wales, young prince Lleu was under a curse that meant he could not take a human wife. His uncle, a magician, came up with an unusual solution; he conjured him up a beautiful bride made from flowers! He called her Blodeuwedd, or "flower face," and for some time the couple were very happy. But when Lleu went away for a few days, the disloyal Blodeuwedd immediately fell in love with another man named Gronw. The underhand pair tried to kill Lleu, but he transformed into an eagle and flew away. The lovers were delighted at his departure, but they didn't enjoy their victory for long. Lleu's uncle found him and restored his human form, and Lleu returned and killed Gronw. At the end of the tale, the uncle turns the treacherous Bloduewedd into an owl, destined to be forever shunned by other birds and to live only by night.

Right Beautiful Blodeuwedd was turned into an owl and doomed to a solitary existence for her faithlessness.

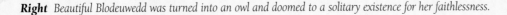

WATER CREATURES

More than 70 percent of the Earth's surface is covered with water, mostly in the form of the vast oceans, whose depths humans haven't yet fully explored. For centuries, sailors have reported seeing strange creatures on the high seas, from mermaids to giant serpents. There are also deep, dark lakes, remote rivers, and underground springs—who is to say what unidentified creatures may lurk in these remote places? Some areas, such as Loch Ness in Scotland and Lake Champlain in Canada, are renowned for sightings of strange, prehistoric-looking creatures, while according to legend rivers and streams conceal a range of monstrous beasts and beautiful water spirits.

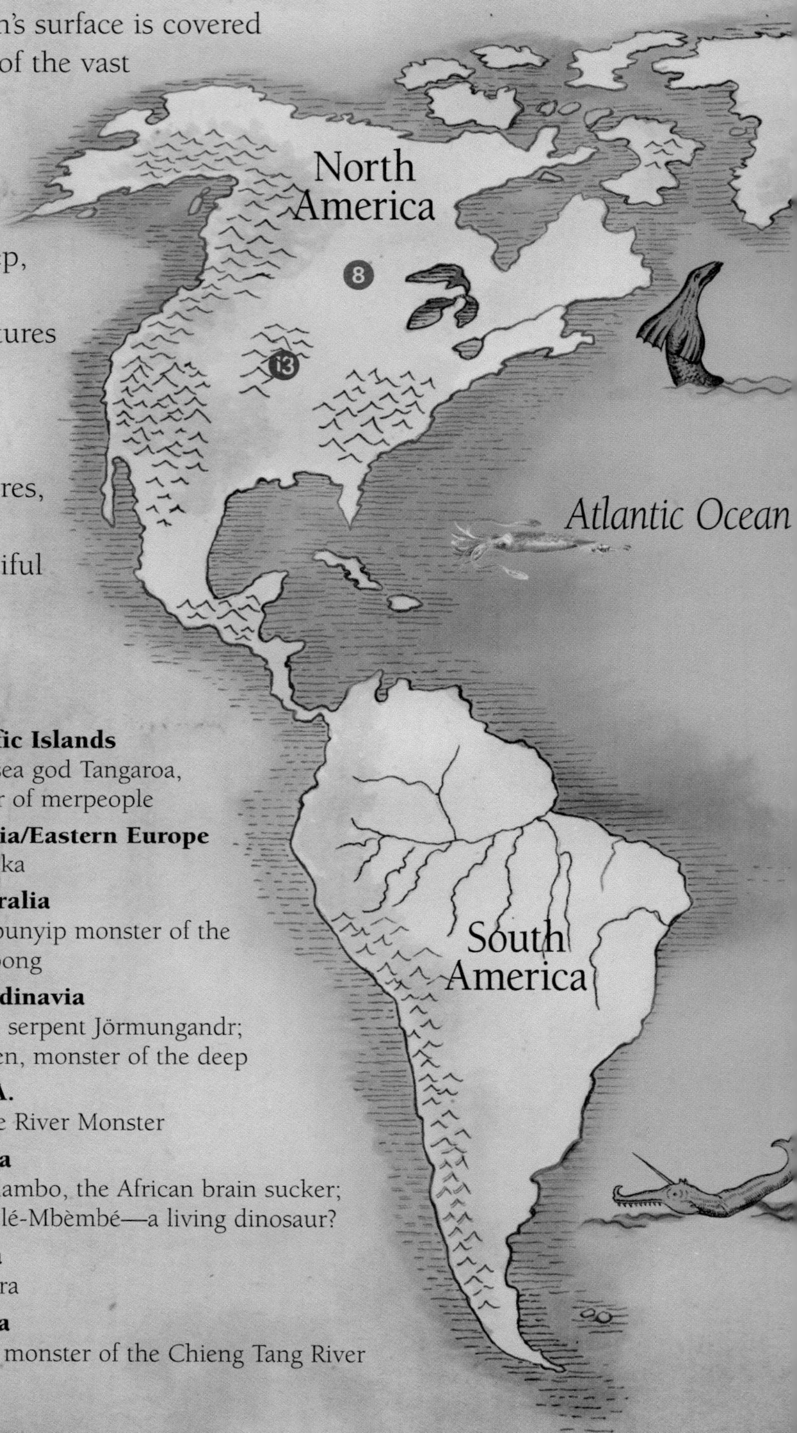

North America

Atlantic Ocean

South America

Worldwide
The Biblical Leviathan, mermaids

1 England
The water demons Peg Powler and Jenny Greenteeth, grindelows

2 Scotland
The famous but elusive Loch Ness Monster

3 Ireland
Merrows

4 Japan
The fish-bodied ningyo

5 Greece
Naiads of rivers, streams, and springs

6 Italy
Scylla and Charybdis, the terrible monsters at the Strait of Messina

7 Germany
Lovelorn Lorelei, the siren; nixes

8 Canada
Lake monsters Champ and Ogopogo

9 Pacific Islands
The sea god Tangaroa, father of merpeople

10 Russia/Eastern Europe
Rusalka

11 Australia
The bunyip monster of the billabong

12 Scandinavia
Giant serpent Jörmungandr; Kraken, monster of the deep

13 U.S.A.
White River Monster

14 Africa
Mamlambo, the African brain sucker; Mokèlé-Mbèmbé—a living dinosaur?

15 India
Makara

16 China
Kiau, monster of the Chieng Tang River

MERMAIDS

Mermaids have cropped up in stories from around the world for centuries. In the myths of the people of the Pacific Islands, for example, humans actually began as merpeople. At the beginning of the world, Tangaroa— god of the sea—gave birth to all the creatures of the oceans including mermen and mermaids, who eventually lost their tails and became human.

I n the folklore of Europe and America mermaids have the head and body of a beautiful maiden and the tail of a fish. They live in the sea, in a splendid underwater world of beautifully adorned palaces overflowing with riches. Mermaids' lives are very long, but the one thing they lack is a soul. Sailors would once tell tales of seeing mermaids sitting on rocks combing their long hair, admiring themselves in mirrors and singing sweet songs.

Mermaids are fascinated by the world of men. Some can even shape-shift, exchanging their tails for legs and coming onto land, where they might seek a human husband. If they do marry a human man, however, their children will have webbed fingers and toes. In some stories mermaids help humans, healing people who are ill for example, but their songs can also lure sailors to their deaths, and their singing is sometimes said to foretell terrible storms.

While mermaids are beautiful, mermen are said to have a terrifying appearance, with green skin and ugly faces. They are wild and uncontrolled, often causing storms and sinking ships. In Irish legend, mermaids are called merrows. The females are alluring and friendly, but male merrows are not: they have green teeth, slit-like eyes, and sharp, red noses.

In Scotland people talk of selkies—seal people who can take on human form. They often marry humans and live on land. But they always keep their seal skin hidden away and when the pull of the sea is very strong, will put it back on to return once again to the water.

Below right Mermaids are renowned for their great beauty and grace, as well as for their fishy tails!

STORM WARNINGS

Japanese mermaids, or ningyo, are friendly and helpful if treated with respect. They have the bodies of huge fish with the heads of beautiful women. Unlike mermaids of the west, they won't lure anyone into danger but will warn humans of danger and ward off any bad luck.

THE LITTLE MERMAID

In this story, by Hans Christian Andersen, a young mermaid falls in love with a human prince, whom she has saved from a shipwreck. She begs a wicked merwitch (a sea witch) to transform her tail into human legs so she can go ashore and be with the prince. The witch agrees but imposes harsh conditions: she takes the mermaid's beautiful voice in payment; she curses her so that every step she takes will be agony; and, worst of all, if the Little Mermaid doesn't make the prince fall in love with her, she will die. Sadly for the Little Mermaid, the prince believes a human princess saved him from drowning. Although he grows to love the Little Mermaid as a sister, he falls in love with and marries the princess instead. The merwitch gives the Little Mermaid one more chance: if she will kill the prince, she can save her own life. But the Little Mermaid cannot do it. Instead, she plunges back into the sea and turns into foam.

Above *"The Little Mermaid" is a fairytale by Hans Christian Andersen. This statue of the Little Mermaid now stands in Copenhagen harbor. Copenhagen, in Denmark, was the home of the author.*

Fantastical fact

Mermaid sightings may actually have been glimpses of sea mammals, such as the dugong or the now-extinct Steller's sea cow.

127

Nixes and Nymphs

While mermaids generally make their home in the sea, nixes and nymphs are creatures of rivers, streams, and lakes. Beautiful but often deadly, these water spirits can lure people to watery deaths.

Peg Powler and Jenny Greenteeth

If ever you are in northern England, be careful near lakes, rivers, millraces, and wells. A wicked being may lurk beneath the surface waiting to drag you under the water. In the River Tees lives Peg Powler, a hideously ugly old woman with green skin, long, lank, green hair and sharp teeth, who grabs the ankles of those who stand too close to the water and pulls them in. Other water demons, such as Jenny Greenteeth and the frightening grindylows, have just the same evil intent; that is, to drown any people, particularly any children, who come too close.

In appearance, nixes of German and Scandinavian folk tales are much like mermaids, with the head and body of a beautiful young girl and the tail of a fish. They can also take human form, but you can always tell them by the hems of their skirts, which are dripping wet. Nixes are known to snatch human babies, replacing them with changelings that are invariably ugly.

In other European myths, nymphs are water spirits. In Greek stories every river, lake, and spring had its own nymph, or naiad. If the water ever dried up, the naiad would die with it. Unlike nixes, naiads had no particular hatred for people. Even so, they could be jealous and dangerous. Hylas, one of the Argonauts (see page 95), was a beautiful

Lorelei

There was once a young maiden named Lorelei, who lived next to the river Rhine in Germany. She was so beautiful that any man who looked into her eyes fell in love with her. Unfortunately, the one man she loved back was unfaithful to her. She wanted to take her own life, but a local bishop stopped her and sent her to live in a convent instead. On the way there, however, she halted at the edge of the cliff overlooking the Rhine, from where she could see the castle of her beloved, and threw herself into the river. At that moment she was transformed into a siren and forever after would sit on a rock combing her long, copper-colored hair and singing enchanting songs, luring sailors to their deaths on the dangerous rocks below.

Right *Tragic Lorelei combs her copper locks and sings her haunting songs. The famous rock where she is said to recline juts out 120 meters above the River Rhine in Germany.*

young man who fascinated a group of naiads he encountered in a spring while fetching water. They enticed him into their watery home, and he was never seen again. When the human lover of a naiad called Nomia was unfaithful to her, she was so enraged that she blinded him. German folklore tells of a knight who married a water nymph only to desert her and marry another woman. But the nymph got her revenge—she made sure that the faithless knight drowned on his wedding day.

RUSALKA

In Russia and Eastern Europe, traditional lore has it that the souls of girls who die violent deaths in or near water become spirits called rusalki: water nymphs who lure men into the water and drown them. Rusalki always have the appearance of beautiful maidens dressed in white. They are usually seen on nights when there is a new moon, singing and dancing in meadows and woodland clearings, drawing men to them. There are apparently two ways you can protect yourself against a rusalka: if you go swimming in the lake where she lives, put a fern in your hair; if you want to help her troubled soul to rest in peace, find out how the ill-fated girl died and avenge her death.

Below Beautiful, white-clad rusalki dance in the woods beneath a new moon, their singing luring the unwary to their deaths.

Below According to the legend, some water nymphs were so enraptured by the beauty of the youth Hylas who came to their spring, that they took him to stay with them forever.

SCYLLA AND CHARYBDIS

The sea has always posed great dangers—storms, whirlpools, giant waves, treacherous reefs, and jagged rocks have all taken the lives of sea-faring adventurers. You are not even safe on land. Floods, tidal surges, and tsunamis all bring destruction from the sea, so it's hardly surprising that the ancient Greeks imagined unspeakable sea monsters.

Above *According to Greek mythology, the twin horrors of Scylla and Charybdis made the Strait of Messina the most dangerous stretch of water in the Mediterranean Sea.*

On opposite sides of the Strait of Messina, between Sicily and the Italian mainland, lay two inescapable terrors. On one side of the strait lived Charybdis, monstrous daughter of Poseidon, who swallowed huge amounts of water three times a day and then spouted it back out again, forming a seething mass of water that swirled in an everlasting whirlpool. Anything that approached Charybdis would be sucked down into the murky depths forever. But to avoid Charybdis meant passing too close to the horror on the other side of the strait: Scylla, the most monstrous creature imaginable, who had twelve legs, a circle of slavering dogs' heads at her waist, and six giant heads on writhing, snake-like necks, which plucked sailors from their boats if they passed within reach beneath her cave.

Two Greek heroes, Odysseus and Jason, successfully faced these monsters. Odysseus, realizing that he had to face one or other of the foes, chose to battle with Scylla. He calculated that, though he risked losing some of his crew, the ship should escape the total destruction it was likely to suffer if they sailed too near to Charybdis. As expected, when the boat steered towards her lair, Scylla appeared. Each of her terrible heads struck at the boat. She snatched up six men, one with each head, but Odysseus managed to navigate out of her reach before she could strike again.

Zeus later wrecked Odysseus' ship in battle and the hero found himself stranded on a raft of wreckage, drifting back towards the Strait of Messina to face the twin horrors of Scylla and Charybdis for a second time. Not daring to risk another encounter with Scylla, he passed near to Charybdis instead. The raft was sucked into the whirlpool, but Odysseus managed to grab onto the branch of a fig tree that overhung the swirling waters. When Charybdis spouted out water again, she expelled his raft with it. Odysseus managed to swim to the raft and paddle away from danger.

The hero Jason had better luck when his ship, the Argo, had to pass through the strait on his return from Colchis, where he had stolen the golden fleece (see page 95). He was protected by the goddess Hera, who sent sea nymphs to sing soothing melodies that quieted the churning waters of Charybdis. The nymphs then guided the Argo away from Scylla's rock so she could not reach it.

Above *Odysseus and his crew navigate perilously close to Scylla in an attempt to avoid the equally dangerous Charybdis. Odysseus lost six men using this strategy, but saved the ship.*

SCYLLA

Scylla was a beautiful sea nymph, beloved by a sea god named Glaucus. Unfortunately for Scylla, although she didn't love Glaucus, the sorceress Circe did, and out of jealousy, Circe poisoned the pool where Scylla went to bathe. As soon as Scylla stepped into the water, she was transformed into a hideous monster. Her heart became filled with loathing. She made her lair at the Strait of Messina, destroying everything that came within her reach.

CHARYBDIS

Charybdis was also a sea nymph. She was the daughter of Poseidon, the chief god of the sea. It was her task to flood dry land for her father, thus increasing his underwater kingdom. One story says that Zeus became angry at this theft of his land and turned Charybdis into a huge monster with a gaping mouth, sucking in water and churning it out again, creating a terrifying whirlpool.

LAKE LURKERS

The elusive monster that is said to lurk in Scotland's Loch Ness is well known, but it is by no means the only lake-dwelling mystery beast. Many lakes are said to harbor unmentionable creatures in their murky depths— here are just a few enigmas from around the world.

Some lakes in the world just seem to attract mystery. Perhaps it's to do with their size or depth or the surrounding landscape. Whatever the reason, it's not difficult to believe that certain lakes could be home to something out of the ordinary. However, sceptics point out that most lake monster sightings have actually turned out to be rather more mundane: swimming deer, otters, seals, driftwood, waves, or optical illusions—even deliberate fakes. Even so, the existence of monsters in lakes across the world is still hotly debated.

Above *This famous 1934 image was revealed as a fake 60 years later. The "monster" turned out to be a plastic neck and head attached to a toy submarine.*

NESSIE

Tales of the Loch Ness monster date back to the time of Saint Columba some 1,600 years ago. The saint is said to have blessed the beast when it emerged from the River Ness— which feeds into the loch—in all its terrible glory. Usually, however, the creature is shy and elusive. Modern interest in the monster was rekindled in the 1930s when a road around the lake was opened, and the creature was spotted several times out of the water, only to lurch back towards the loch again when it was disturbed. It was said to be large and bulky with a long neck and a small head. Some people have suggested that the creature might be a surviving plesiosaur—a giant marine reptile that became extinct at the same time as the dinosaurs. Various sonar readings, photographs, and snippets of footage of the "monster" have built up over the years and various investigations have sought to examine the claims. Between 1962 and 1972 there was even a Loch Ness Investigation Bureau. Despite all this interest, Nessie remains elusive and unexplained.

CHAMP AND OGOPOGO

A creature called Champ is said to live in Lake Champlain, a large lake on the border between Canada (Quebec) and the U.S.A. (New York state and Vermont). Champ was first spotted as early as 1609 by the French explorer Samuel de Champlain. Since then there have been over 300 reported sightings. A lake monster also appears in the legends of the local native peoples, the Iroquois and the Abenaki. Whether or not Champ actually exists, he is certainly a great tourist attraction. The lakeside village of Port Henry even holds a "Champ Day" every August!

Lake Okanogan of British Columbia, also in Canada, is thought to be home to a lake monster nicknamed Ogopogo, though the native people prefer the more respectful N'haitaka, which means "water demon." Like other lake monsters it is said to resemble a plesiosaur, with a streamlined body, long neck, and small head. Unauthenticated photographs and film footage of the creature exist, but nothing has been proven.

Below *A serpentine figure glides silently across a still lake surface in the dawn mist. But do such lake lurkers really exist, or are they just figments of people's feverish imagination?*

Above *Frightened Aborignal Australians flee from a terrifying bunyip. This mysterious and bloodthirsty monster is said to haunt waterholes in the arid Australian outback.*

AUSTRALIA'S BUNYIP

In a dry country like Australia, lakes, billabongs, and waterholes are vital sources of water. But no matter how great your need for water, always be careful when approaching a waterhole there. A bunyip, a creature of Aboriginal legend, might live below the surface. No one quite knows what these lake creatures look like, but their name means "devil" or "spirit," and everyone agrees that they can be dangerous. Many have described the bunyip as having dark fur, a dog-like face, flippers, tusks, and the tail of a horse. Bunyips are reputed to be shy and elusive, but if provoked, they can become fierce man-killers, emerging from the water at night to devour any creature, animal or human, who comes near. Many explanations for the bunyip have been suggested over the years. Some say they are seals that have swum up-river from the sea, others that they are tribal memories of long-extinct giant marsupials that roamed Australia when humans first arrived.

MONSTERS OF THE DEEP

What lurks in the deep oceans, where sunlight never reaches? Even today we do not know everything about the life that exists in the ocean depths. Hundreds of years ago, we knew even less and imagined even more …

Above *With suckered arms as broad as tree trunks, a terrible, squid-like sea monster attacks a ship. For centuries sailors have told tales of creatures such as this.*

Huge, scaly, and unstoppable—massive sea serpents have been described by sea-faring people worldwide for centuries. They appear in the mythology and folk tales of Scandinavia, the Mediterranean, and the Near East. Even the Bible has its fair share of sea monsters. Norse myths feature a particularly massive sea serpent. Jörmungandr, the Midgard Serpent, was so long that it encircled the entire world, and sailors mistook the humps on its back for islands.

In some accounts sea serpents were snakelike, while in others they were more like sea dragons, with horns on their heads and whiskers. Some, like the Leviathan, were even said to breathe fire. Ancient Greek writers took stories about sea serpents very seriously and kept careful records of apparent eye-witness accounts. Since then there have been hundreds of reported sightings, and unlike many sightings of weird animals, sightings of sea monsters are often reported by several people at the same time. However, despite at least 1,200 sightings having been documented over the years, there is still no real evidence for the actual existence of such underwater beasts.

KRAKEN

A terrifying sea monster of Scandinavian folklore and legend, the Kraken was described as being the size of a floating island. It created dangerous whirlpools and dragged passing ships down to the bottom of the ocean. Kraken was sometimes said to have the appearance of a giant crab, other times that of a gargantuan octopus or squid. The legendary beast has inspired many fictional sea monsters, including the terrible giant squid in Jules Verne's classic book *Twenty Thousand Leagues Under the Sea*.

LEVIATHAN

Leviathan is a terrible sea monster mentioned several times in the Bible's Old Testament. Leviathan was over 900 miles (1,450 km) long and circled the Earth in the ocean depths. It breathed fire from its mouth and smoke from his nostrils and made the sea boil around it—no weapon could harm it. It was sometimes described as having 7 heads and 300 eyes. Some stories say that God created Leviathan to play with; others

Above *Leviathan, massive sea monster of the Old Testament, faces Hebrew god Yahweh in a monumental battle in the waters of chaos.*

describe how Yahweh, the god of the Hebrews, fought Leviathan in the waters of chaos and finally killed it. That is not the last the world will see of the Leviathan, however. According to the Bible, on the Day of Judgement the monster will be served up and consumed as part of a great feast.

REAL-LIFE MONSTERS OF THE DEEP

Terrible storms, giant waves, glimpses of whales and walruses, the unearthly glow of phosphorescent creatures, and the shadows of massive shoals of fish might all have fuelled tales of sea monsters. But sometimes fact is stranger even than fiction. There are real-life sea monsters that are equally if not more terrifying than their legendary counterparts. The giant squid, for example, which might have inspired Kraken stories, was only known from a few incomplete specimens and unauthenticated sightings until 2004, when one was finally photographed for the first time. This specimen was a massive 8 meters (26 ft) long. Scientists estimate that giant squids can grow up to 14 meters (46 ft) in length; that's longer than most buses. A likely candidate for the legendary sea serpent is the oar fish—the largest bony fish in the world, which can reach lengths of up to 11 meters (36 ft). Its silver body, bright-red dorsal fin, and the mane-like crest behind its head give it a strange and unearthly appearance.

Below *A giant squid would dwarf the average diver. But rather than sailors and their ships, this monster feeds on fish and other squid.*

135

RIVER MONSTERS

Rivers are home to some of the world's deadliest creatures, including crocodiles and piranhas. But what other terrors might they conceal in their highest reaches and darkest depths? Many rivers around the world are said to harbor their own supernatural horrors.

China has many tales of river monsters. One legend tells of a great serpent that lived in the Chieng Tang river. This ferocious creature, known as Kiau, terrorized the people and was clever too. Although over 100 meters (328 ft) long, it was able to camouflage itself—no one knew where it was or when it might strike, which made it very difficult to fight. The monster was finally killed by a local hero in a monumental battle. The Makara of Hindu mythology is a monster of rivers and waters. It has a tortoise's body, an elephant's trunk, the mouth and teeth of a crocodile, and a fish's tail; and its name means "creature that is neither one thing nor another!" In one legend Ganga, goddess of rivers, rode on the back of the Makara down to the sea, spreading fertility across the land and making rice grow. Varuna, god of winds, also rides the Makara.

Above With an evil glint in its eye, the Chieng Tang serpent emerges from its watery lair.

RIVER MONSTERS TODAY

For almost 100 years the people of Newport, Arkansas, U.S.A., have reported seeing an unidentified beast thrashing about in White River, which runs through their town. At 4–7 meters long (13–23 ft) it is quite a giant and, judging by the strange tracks found on the banks of the river, it seems to be just as at home on land. Some people have dismissed the creature as a displaced seal or even a penguin! Others think it is a large fish, such as a paddlefish or a sturgeon. Eye-witnesses say the beast has smooth, gray skin, a large, gaping mouth and, most unusual of all, a long protuberance sticking out from its head.

Above *With the mouth and teeth of a crocodile and the trunk of an elephant, the Hindu Makara certainly deserves its name of "neither one thing nor another"!*

The Mzintiava River in South Africa is home to a strange creature called a Mamlambo, or African Brain Sucker. It is described as half-horse and half-fish and over 20 meters (66 ft) long with short legs, a body like a crocodile, and a snake-like head. It has a hypnotic stare, and its eyes shine green at night. The Mamlambo is dangerous as well as terrifying to look at. People who live in the area say it has dragged animals and humans into the water, where it sucks out their blood and brains. Local police believe the deaths are normal drowning accidents, but many people still believe that the river monster exists. Legend has it that if anyone is ever brave enough to capture the Mamlambo, great wealth will come to them.

MOKÈLÉ-MBÈMBÉ—A LIVING DINOSAUR?

About 100 years ago people from a small village in the heart of the Congo jungle in Central Africa started reporting sightings of a very strange animal in or near the Congo River: a large creature, about the size of an elephant, with brown or gray skin, a long neck and tail, and a small head. Several foreigners also reported having seen the creature. All of the descriptions matched that of the extinct dinosaur, Apatosaurus. Although the real dinosaur was a plant eater, local people said this creature had

attacked people. They linked it with ancient rock paintings nearby, which showed a long-necked, four-footed beast known as mokèlé-mbèmbé, meaning "rainbow." Since these early sightings, scientific investigations have brought back specimens of droppings and casts of huge footprints. But despite these findings and other evidence, the existence of the mokèlé-mbèmbé has yet to be proven.

Left *An artist's impression of the mokèlé mbèmbé browsing peacefully in the forest. Is it a living dinosaur or a figment of the imagination?*

GLOSSARY

afterlife The life that coninues after death in the beliefs of many cultures, ancient and modern.

alchemy The practice of early scientific experiments to discover the secret of everlasting life or to turn ordinary metals into gold.

astrology The study of stars and planets and how, some people believe, they affect human lives.

Babylon An ancient city and capital of Babylonia—a kingdom that covered part of modern day Iraq.

Brothers Grimm German brothers Jacob and Wilhelm, who collected and published a collection of European folktales in the 19th century.

Camelot The location of the court of King Arthur in British legends.

canopic jars Containers, used to store internal organs, that ancient Egyptians buried with mummified bodies.

cryptozoology The study of creatures whose existence is not proven, such as the yeti, sasquatch, and Loch Ness Monster.

Day of Judgement According to many religious beliefs, the end of the world, when all souls will be judged for their actions.

demon An evil being or spirit.

ectoplasm A supernatural substance associated with the appearance or presence of ghosts.

exorcism The casting out of demons that are possessing a person or animal.

extinction The death of all members of a species. Extinct species are irretrievably lost.

familiars Demons in the shape of animals that were believed to accompany witches.

folklore The traditional beliefs, myths, tales, and customs of a community, handed down by storytelling.

heroes In the myths of many countries, particularly Greece and Rome, heros were men of supreme strength and ability who performed acts of great bravery.

immortal Fated to live forever and unable to die.

ka A person's life force in the beliefs of the ancient Egyptians.

labors of Hercules A series of twelve seemingly impossible tasks set for the ancient Greek hero Hercules (or Herakles) by King Eurystheus.

legends Stories handed down from earlier times, sometimes originally based in historical fact but usually much changed.

levitation The raising of people or objects into the air by the power of the mind alone.

marsupials Mammals that nurses their young in a pouch, such as native Australian kangaroos, koalas, and possums.

Mesopotamia An ancient land in the Middle East between the rivers Tigris and Euphrates (now a region in modern day Iraq). Mesopotamia means "between rivers."

Middle Ages The period of history dating from roughly 500–1500AD. Described as medieval.

mortal Human and capable of dying.

Muses Goddesses of ancient Greece who controlled the arts and sciences.

myths Traditional, ancient stories dealing with supernatural beings, monsters, gods, and heroes. Myths often explain aspects of the natural world, such as the existence of mountains and rivers.

natron A naturally occurring mineral salt (hydrated sodium carbonate) that is effective at drying out materials—used in embalming and mummification by the ancient Egyptians.

Norse Relating to the people of Scandinavia, particularly Norway, in medieval times.

paranormal not scientifically explainable.

parapsychology The study of psychological phenomena not explained by current science, such as telepathy.

psychology The study of the mind and behavior.

Persia An ancient Middle Eastern country—modern day Iran.

phenomenon A notable event or happening, often one that is unexplained The plural is phenomena.

Phoenicia An ancient Middle Eastern country roughly equivalent in territory to modern day Syria and Lebanon.

phosphorescence Natural light that a substance or animal emits without producing heat.

prophecy A foretelling of the future.

psychic relating to skills or phenomena that are unexplained by natural processes or scientific understanding, especially telepathy and telling the future.

psychokinesis The movement of objects by the power of the mind.

Puritan A follower of a strict type of Christianity that was common in England and on the east coast of North America in the 1600s.

Santa Claus Also known as Father Christmas or Saint Nicholas; a popular Christmas figure in Western nations.

Satan One of many names used for the Devil in Christian and Jewish belief.

scarab A type of dung beetle that was sacred to the ancient Egyptians.

sonar A system for detecting objects underwater using sound waves.

supernatural Something, such as ghosts, that cannot be explained by known natural processes.

Trojan War A legendary war between Greece and Troy (an ancient kingdom sited in present day Turkey).

tsunami A huge ocean wave caused by the displacement of sea water offshore, for example by an underwater earthquake or volcanic eruption.

underworld The land of the dead, which is said in many cultures to exist beneath the surface of the Earth.

Voudou (Voodoo) A religion practiced in some Caribbean countries, particularly Haiti—a combination of native African and Roman Catholic beliefs.

Wicca A religion that centers on the worship of nature, including deities of the sun and moon. Practitioners sometimes describe themselves as witches.

World War I and World War II Conflicts that took place between 1914–1918 and 1939–1945 and involved most of the major nations of the world.

zodiac A band of the heavens divided into twelve controlling "houses"—the signs of the zodiac. Some people believe that they affect human lives.

FURTHER READING

BOOKS

Allen, J. (2005) *Fantasy Encyclopedia*
London, Kingfisher

Andersen. H. C. (2004) *Andersen's Fairy Tales*
Maryland, Wildside Press

Buller, L. (2003) *Myths and Monsters from Dragons to Werewolves* London, Dorling Kindersley

Dedopulos, T. (2001) *Wizards: A Magical History Tour* London, Carlton Books

Dowswell, P., Greenwood, S. (2003) *Witches* London, Anness Publishing Ltd

Gee, J. (2007) *Encyclopedia Horrifica: The Terrifying TRUTH! About Vampires, Ghosts, Monsters and More* New York, Scholastic Inc

Brothers Grimm, Cruikshank, G. (1996) *Grimms' Fairy Tales* New York, Penguin Group U.S.A.

Mason, P. (2004) *Investigating the Supernatural* Chicago, Heinemann

Matthews, C., Matthews, J. (2005) *The Element Encyclopedia of Magical Creatures* New York, Barnes & Noble

Penner, L. R., Scott, P. (2004) *Dragons* New York, Random House Children's Books

Philip, N. (2005) *Mythology* New York, DK Publishing Inc

Rose, C. (2001) *Giants, Monsters, and Dragons: An Encyclopedia of Folklore, Legend, and Myth* New York, W.W. Norton & Company Inc

Stefof, R. (2007) *Witches and Witchcraft* Singapore, Marshall Cavendish Inc

Torpie, K., Deen, D. (2007) *Mythical Beasts* Connecticut, Innovative Kids

Woodside, M., Corvino, L., Pober, A. (2008) *Arabian Nights* New York, Sterling Publishing

WEBSITES

www.wikipedia.org
Wikipedia provides information on just about everything and is a great place to start your research. But anyone can add information, so check out other resources too.

www.newanimal.org
This site is like an online zoo for weird and wonderful animals that might or might not be real, such as the Loch Ness Monster, the yeti, and the Mongolian death worm.

www.blackdrago.com
Visit *The Circle of the Dragon* for information on everything to do with dragons and for some great images.

www.mythencyclopedia.com
From Aladdin to zombies—myths and legends of the world are arranged in alphabetical order in this online encyclopedia, so it's easy to find your favorite.

www.pantheon.org
Encyclopedia Mythica: short articles packed with information on mythology, folklore, and religion across the world. There are plenty of pictures, too.

www.unknownexplorers.com
Do you want to find out about ghosts, aliens, and the paranormal? *Unknown Explorers* is the Internet's central hub for exploring unknown phenomena.

INDEX

Page numbers in *italics* refer to illustrations.

A

abominable snowman 58, 62
Aeetes, King of Colchis 95
Aegeus, King of Athens 81
Aepyornis maximus see elephant bird
African Brain Sucker 137
Aladdin 38
Alberich 24, 25
alchemists/alchemy 35
Alexander the Great 102
alicorns 75
Ammut 98, 106–7
Andersen, Hans Christian: "The Little Mermaid" 127
animals *see* cats; dogs; familiars; foxes
Anubis 98, 106, 107
ape-men 62–3
Apophis 86, 88
Arabian Nights 38, 39
Argonauts, the 95, 129, 131
Ariadne 80, 81
Ariosto, Ludovico 103
Arthur, King 28, 36–7, 103
Arzshenk 72, 81
Askeladden (Ash Lad) 67
Asmodeus 56
Astaroth 56
Atargatis 124
"automatic" writing 40
aziza 8, 11

B

Baal 56
Baba Yaga 28, 31
banshees 44, 54–5
barbegazi 8, 27
Barguest 98, 110
Bean Nighe *see* washer women

"Beauty and the Beast" 67
Beelzebub 56
Belial 56
Bellerophon 76–7
Bida 86, 88
bigfoot 58, 63
black arts 43
Black Shuck 98, 110
Blodeuwedd 112, 123
boggarts 8, 18–19
Bokwus 58, 70
Book of One Thousand and One Nights, The 38, 39
broomsticks 30, 31
brownies 8, 16–17
Buffy the Vampire Slayer 47
bulls, sacred 81
bunyips 124, 133

C

Carnarvon, George Herbert, 5th Earl of 48
Carter, Howard 48
cats 30, 100
 vampire cats 98, 100–1
Cau'd Lad of Hylton 21
cauldrons 30, 31
centaurs 72, 79, 82–3
Cerberus 98, 108–9
Chamber Hall, Oldham, England: boggart 19
Champ 124, 132
Charon 108
Charybdis 131
 see Scylla and Charybdis
Chieng Tang serpent *136*
Chimera 76, 77, 98
Chiron 82–3
Circe 30, 31
conjurers 34, 35
corpse candles 54
corpse dogs 110
corpse lights 54
Cottingley fairies, the 13
Cu Sith 98, 110

curinqueans 58, 63
Cwm Annwyn hounds 98, 110
cyclopes 58, 64

D

Dahl, Roald 23
 The Gremlins 23
Danaë 69
Dartmoor, Beast of 98, 111
Death worm 86, 91
deathly spirits 54–5
Dee, Dr John 28, 35
Deianeira 83
demons 35, 44, 56–7
Devil, the (Satan) 33, 54, 56, *89*
Devil's Dandy 110
Dionysus 84
Disney, Walt 23
divining 34
diwata 8, 11
djinn 28, 38–39
dogs 110
 black hounds 110
 Black Shuck 98, 110
 corpse dogs 110
 Cwm Annwyn hounds 98, 110
 Gabriel Hounds 98, 110
 see also were-dogs
domovoi 8, 17
Doyle, Sir Arthur Conan 13
Dracula, Count 44, 46, 47
dragons 86, 88–9
 Chinese 89, 90, *91*
 Greek 94–5
 Japanese 89, 92–3
 Welsh 88
 see also George, St.
Dronsfield, James: *Ouselwood 19*
Dryope 85
dugongs 127
Dullahan 44, 55
dwarves 8, 24–5
Dzoavits 58, 65

E

each uisgé 72, 79
ectoplasm 40
ein saung nat *see* nats
elephant bird 112, 119
Elizabeth I, Queen of England 35
elves 8, 14, 24
enchanters 35
enchantresses 30–1
ergot poisoning 61
erlkings 8, 20
Eurystheus, King of Tiryns 108
evil spirits 44
exorcism 56, *57*

F

Fafnir 97
fairies 8, 10
 winged fairies 8, 12–13
fakirs 34
familiars 30, *33*, 57
fauns 72, 84, *85*
Faustus, Dr 28, *35*
fenghuang 112, 115
firebirds 112, 115
"Fisherman and the Djinni, The" 38, 39
Flamel, Nicolas 28, 35
Fox Sisters, Kate and Margaret 28, 41
foxes, vampire 98, 101
foxfire 54
fox spirits 44, 101
Frankenstein 50, *51*
furies 58, 69

G

Gabble Ratchets 110
Gabriel Hounds 98, 110
Ganga 136
Garuda 112, 120
genies 38
George, St., and the dragon 96–7
ghosts 44, 52–3
giants 58, 64–5
Glashtyn 72

Glaucus 131
gnomes 8, 26–7
  garden gnomes 27
Gob, King of the Gnomes 27
goblins 8, 20–1
golems 44, 50–1
gorgons 58, 68–9
Grandier, Father Urbaine 57
Green Man 58, 70, *70*, *71*
Green George *see* Green Man
Green Jack *see* Green Man
gremlins 8, 22–3
Grey Ones 68, 69
griffins 98, 102–3
Griffiths, Frances 13, *27*
Grimm, Brothers 23, *30*
grimoires 57
Gurt Dog 110
Gwyn ap Nudd 110
Gytrash 110

H
Hades 108
hallucinations 61
Han-Riu 92
Hansel and Gretel 30
harpies 58, 68
headless horsemen 55
Heinzelmännchen 16
Hercules (Herakles) 83, 94, *95*, 108
Hermes 85
Herne the Hunter 58, 71
hippogriffs 98, 103
hobby lanterns 54
hobs 16
Hodgson, B. H. 62
Homo floresiensis 62
ho-oo 112, 115
Hopkins, Matthew, Witchfinder General 28, 33
Howard-Bury, Charles 62
Hreidmar 97
Hu-hsein 98, 101
Hydra 86, 94, *95*

Hylas 129
Hylton Castle, Tyne and Wear, England: Cau'd Lad of 21

I
illusions 34, 35
Iobates, King of Lycia 76
Itō Sōda 100–1

J
"Jack and the Beanstalk" 65
Jack-in-the-Green *see* Green Man
jack-o'-lanterns 44, 54
Jason and the Golden Fleece 95, 131
Jenny Greenteeth 124, 128
Jinn, the 38
Jörmungandr 124, 134

K
Ka 106
Kali 44, 46
Ka-Riu 92
Karloff, Boris *51*
kelpies 72, 78, 79
kere 72, 74, 75
Kiau 124
kirin 72, 75
kitsune 54, *101*
kitsunebi 44, 54
Kraken 124, 134–5
Kujata 72, 81

L
Ladon 86, 94
Lakshmi 120
Leaf King *see* Green Man
"Legend of Sleepy Hollow, The" 55
leprechauns 8, 14
Leviathan 124, 134, 135
levitation 34, 40
Lewis, C. S.: *The Lion, the Witch and the Wardrobe* 82, *82*, 84, *85*

Lilith 44, 46
little people 8
Lleu, Prince 123
Loch Ness Monster 124, 132
Loki 97
Lorelei 124, 128
Loudon, nuns of 57
Lucifer 56
lung (Chinese dragon) 86, 90
"Lusmore and the Fairies" 12–13
lycanthropes *60*

M
Macan Gadungan 58, 60
Maezt Dar l'Oudou 38
mages 35
magicians 34
Makara 124, 136
Mamadi 88
Mamlambo 124, 137
manananggal 28, 31
manticores 98, 105
Medea 95
mediums 40
Medusa 68, 69
Melusine 8, *11*
Merlin 28, 36–7, 88
mermaids 124, 126–7
mermen 124, 126
merrows 124
Midgard Serpent *see* Jörmungandr
Minos, King of Crete 80
Minotaur, the 72, 80–1
Mokèlé-Mbèmbé 124, 137
mummies 44, 48–9
Mummy, The (film) 49
Mummy's Curse, The (film) 49
mystics 28, 35
  Chinese 34

N
naiads 124, 128, 129
nang-lha 8, 20–1

Narcisse, Clairvius 51
nats *17*
  ein saung nat 8, *17*
nature worshippers 43
necromancers 35
nee-gued 58, 62
Nessus 83
neugles 72, 79
N'haitaka 133
nickurs 72, 79
Night of the Demon (film) 57
Nimue 28, *36*, 37
ningyo 124, 126
nisse 8, 16, 17
nixes 124, 128
Nomia 129
Nosferatu (film) 47
nymphs 124, 128, 129

O
oar fish 135
Oberon *13*
Odin 77
Odysseus 31, 64, 122–3, 131
Oedipus 104
o-gon-cho 92
Ogopogo 124, 133
ogres 58, 66–7
oni 58, 66–7
Orpheus 122
Otr 97
owl maiden 112

P
Pan 85
Paracelsus 26
Parris, Betty 32
patupairehe 8, 11
Peg Powler 124, 128
Pegasus 72, 76–7
peri 8, *10*, 11
Perseus 69
"philosopher's stone" 35
Phineas 68
phoenix 112, 114
piskies *see* pixies
pixies 8, 11

Pliny the Elder 74
poh 72, 75
Polo, Marco 74, 118, 119
poltergeists 41, 44
Polydectes, King of Seriphos 69
Polyphemus 64
pooka 72, 78
possession 56, 57
Potter, Harry *see* Rowling, J. K.
psychokinesis 41
Ptah 72, 81

Q
qilin 72, 75, *75*
Questing Beast 98, 103
Quetzalcoatl 86, 88
Qur'an 38

R
Rackham, Arthur: *Oberon and Titania 13*
Rainbow Serpent 86, 89
Raven 112, 117
Regin 97
Richard II, King 71
Ri-Riu 92
roc 112, 118, 119
Rowling, J. K.: Harry Potter books *18*, 37, 103
Rübezahl 27
rukhs *see* roc
Rumpelstiltskin 24, 25
rusalki 124, 129
Rustam 81
ryu 86, 92

S
sabbats *33*
Salem witches 28, 32–3
Santa Claus 14
sasquatch 58, 63
Satan *see* Devil, the
satyrs 72, 84–5
Scheherazade 39
Schreck, Max *47*

Scylla and Charybdis 124, 130–1
séances 40, 41
Seiryuu 93
Sekhmet 46
selkies 126
serou 72, 75
Shahnameh, the *120*
Shamanism/shamans 28, 4–3
Inuit 42, 43
Navaho skinwalkers 61
shape-shifters 30–1, 57, 78–9, 101, 117, 126
Shipton, Eric 62
Shrek (film) *67*
sidhe 8
Sigurd 97
Silenus 84
Simurgh 112, 120, *121*
"Sindbad the Sailor" 38, 118
sirens 112, 122–3
sirin 112, 123
skinwalkers, Navajo 30, 58, 61
sleight of hand 34
Sleipnir 72, 77
snake charmers 34
sorcerers 35
spell-casting 31, 34
sphinxes
Egyptian 98, 104
Greek 98, 104
spirit guides 40
spiritualism/spiritualists 28, 40–1
spirit walkers 28
squids, giant 135
Steller's sea cows 127
Stoker, Bram: *Dracula* 46, 47
Sui-Riu 92
Susa-no-o 96
Syrinx 85

T
Tangaroa 124
Tano Giant 58, 62–3

tatsu 86, 92
telekinesis *41*
Thaumas *68*
Theseus 80–1
Thoth 106, *107*
Thunderbird 112, 116–17
thunderhorses 72, 83
Titania *13*
Tituba 32, 33
Tolkien, J. R. R.
The Hobbit 14, 37
The Lord of the Rings 14, 37
tomte *see* nisse
totem poles *117*
trolls 58, 66–7
tsopou 72, 75
Tutankhamun 48

U
unicorns 72, 74–5
Uther Pendragon 36

V
vættir 27
vampire cats 98, 100–1
vampire foxes 98, 101
vampires 44, 46, 61
Verne, Jules: *Twenty Thousand Leagues Under the Sea* 135
vidyeshvaras 8, 11
Vishnu 120
Viviane *see* Nimue
Vlad III ("the Impaler") 44, 47
Vortigern, King of Britain 88
Voodoo *see* Voudou
Voudou 28, 33, 50, 51

W
Waheela 98, 109
warlocks 30
washer women, doom-bringing 44, 55
water creatures 124
water horses 72, 78–9
Wendigo 58, 67

were-dogs 58, 60
werewolves 44, 58, 60–1
White River Monster 124, 137
Wicca/Wiccans 43
Wilde, Oscar: *The Selfish Giant* 64
Wild Hunt 98, 110
will-o'-the-wisps 44, 54
Windsor Great Park, England 71
Wisht Hound 110
witches 28, 30–1, 56–7
Salem witches 28, 32–3
witch doctors 28
witch-hunting 32, 33
wizards 28, 34–5, 57
Woden's Hunt 98, 110
wolves *see* Waheela; werewolves
women, monstrous 68–9
see also washer women; witches
Wonambi naracoortensi 89
woodland beings 70
"worms" 86
Wright, Elsie 13, *27*
wushu 34

Y
yeh-teh *63*
yeti 58, 62
Ymir 14

Z
Zal 120
Zeus 76, 77, 81, 82, 131
zombies 35, 44, 50

ACKNOWLEDGMENTS

The publisher thanks the following agencies and illustrators for their kind permission to use their images.

Cover: Front Mary Evans Picture Library, Fotolia, akg-images/Peter Connolly, iStock, Paul Robinson; **F. flap** Fotolia, Ashley Nagy; **Back** iStock, Paul Robinson; **B. flap** Fotolia/Robert Mobley, Gill Tomblin, Ronald Grant Archives/© Warner Bros & J K Rowling

Pages: 2-3 Marshall Editions Archive; **5, 10, 11t, 11b** Mary Evans Picture Library; **13t, 14t** The Bridgeman Art Library; **13b** Topfoto/Fortean; **14b** Corbis/Swim Ink; **15** The Kobal Collection; **16** Mary Evans Picture Library; **17t** The Bridgeman Art Library; **17b** Corbis/Michael Freeman; **18** Ronald Grant Archives/© Warner Bros & J K Rowling; **19t** Fotolia; **19b** Tofoto/HIP/The Print Collector; **20, 21t** Mary Evans Picture Library; **23** Topfoto/KPA; **24** Mary Evans Picture Library; **25b** The Bridgeman Art Library; **26** The Art Archive/Bibliothèque des Arts Décoratifs Paris/Gianni Dagli Orti; **27t** Topfoto; **27b** iStock; **30** Mary Evans Picture Library; **31t** Fotolia; **30-31**Fotolia; **31b, 32** The Bridgeman Art Library; **33t** The Bridgeman Art Library/Museo Lazaro Galdiano, Madrid; **33b** The Bridgeman Art Library/Private Collection; **34** Topfoto/The Granger Collection; **35t** akg-images; **35b** Bridgeman Art Library/Lauros/Giraudon/Musee de Tesse, Le Mans; **36** Scala, Florence/White Images; **37t** The Kobal Collection; **37b** Ronald Grant Archives/© Warner Bros & J K Rowling; **38, 39br, 40** Mary Evans Picture Library; **40tc, 40c** Quarto Group; **41b, 41t** Mary Evans Picture; Library; **42** The Bridgeman Art Library/Krasnoyarskiy Kraevoy Musey, Krasnoyarsk, Russia; **43t** Werner Forman Archives/formerly G.Terasaki Collection, NY; **43b** Corbis/The Cover Story/Floris Leeuwenberg; **46-47** Corbis/Bettman Archives; **46l** Doubleday, 1902; **47t** Getty Images; **47b** The Kobal Collection/20th Century Fox Television/Jerry Wolf; **48l** Corbis/Bettman Archives; **48r** Corbis/Hulton-Deutsch Collection; **49t** Advertising Archives; **50** The Bridgeman Art Library/Private Collection; **50-51** Corbis/Bettmann; **51c** The Kobal Collection; **52b** Mary Evans Picture Library; **52-53** The Bridgeman Art Library/Archives Charmet/Bibliotheque des Arts Decoratifs, Paris; **53b** Topfoto; **54** Mary Evans Picture Library; **55b** Scala, Florence/Smithsonian American Art Museum; **56** The Bridgeman Art Library/The Detroit Institute of Arts, USA/Founders Society purchase with Mr & Mrs Bert L. Smokler & Mr & Mrs Lawrence A. Fleischman funds; **57t** The Kobal Collection/Columbia; **57b** The Bridgeman Art Library/Archives Charmet/Bibliotheque Nationale, Paris; **60** iStock; **61t** The Art Archive; **62** Getty Images; **63t** Corbis/Bettmann; **64** The Art Archive; **65t** The Art Archive/© Henry Matthew Brock; **65b** akg-images/Peter Connolly; **66** Mary Evans Picture Library; **67t** The Kobal Collection/Dreamworks LLC; **67b** Mary Evans Picture Library; **68** Mary Evans Picture Library; **69** Scala, Florence/Galleria degli Uffizi; **70** Mary Evans Picture Library; **71b** Getty Images/Mansell Collection/Time Life; **74** akg-images; **75** akg-images/ Bruce Connolly; **76-77** The Bridgeman Art Library/Private Collection/Look and Learn; **77r** Mary Evans Picture Library; **78** Topfoto/Fortean; **80** The Bridgeman Art Library/Private Collection; **81b** The Bridgeman Art Library/Louvre, Paris; **82** The Ronald Grant Archives/© Disney Enterprises; **83** akg-images/Musée des Beaux-Arts; **84-85** The Art Archive/Art Gallery of New South Wales; **85t** The Bridgeman Art Library/The Stapleton Collection; **85b** Ronald Grant Archives/Waldron Media © Disney; **88t** iStock; **88-89** The Kobal Collection/Paramount/Shangri-la; **91l** Fotolia/Luisafer; **91r** Fotolia/Dan Marsh; **92-93** Corbis/Philadelphia Museum of Art; **93b** Utagawa Kuniyoshi/Public domain/http://commons.wikimedia.org; **94** Corbis/Araldo de Luca; **95t** The Bridgeman Art Library/Private Collection; **95b** akg-images/Peter Connolly; **96** Utagawa Kuniyoshi/Public Domain/http://commons.wikimedia.org; **97t** Topfoto/Roger Viollet; **100-101** Fotolia/Robert Mobley; **101b** Corbis/Asian Art & Archaeology, Inc; **102** The Bridgeman Art Library/ Private Collection/Look and Learn; **103t** iStock; **103b** Topfoto/Charles Walker; **104-105** Mary Evans Picture Library; **105t** The Art Archive; **106t** The Bridgeman Art Library/British Museum, London; **106b** The Bridgeman Art Library/Egyptian National Museum, Cairo; **107** Corbis/Theo Allofs; **107b** Mary Evans Picture Library; **108** Corbis/Christie's Images; **109t** The Bridgeman Art Library/Ashmolean Museum, University of Oxford; **109b** Corbis/Zefa/Alan & Sandy Carey; **110** Mary Evans Picture Library; **111r** The Bridgeman Art Library; **111c** Fortean Picture Library; **114br** The Bridgeman Art Library/Allans of Duke Street, London; **116-117** Corbis/Ron Sanford; **117cl** Corbis/Ron Watts; **117cr** © Gerald McDermott, from A Trickster Tale from the Pacific Northwest published by Harcourt; **118** The Bridgeman Art Library/Private Collection/Look and Learn; **119t** DK Images; **118-119** The Bridgeman Art Library/British Library, London; **120** Corbis/Christie's Images; **121** The Bridgeman Art Library/The Trustees of the Chester Beatty Library, Dublin; **122** The Bridgeman Art Library/National Gallery of Victoria, Melbourne; **123t** Public Domain/Birds of Joy and Sorrow, 1896 by Viktor Vasnetsov/http://commons.wikimedia.org; **126-127** The Art Archive/Private Collection / Marc Charmet; **127t** Corbis/Dave Bartruff; **128** The Bridgeman Art Library/Archives Charmet/ Bibliotheque des Arts Decoratifs, Paris; **129t** Public Domain/Rusalki by Witold Pruszkowski/http://commons.wikimedia.org; **129b** The Bridgeman Art Library/Manchester Art Gallery; **130** akg-images/Erich Lessing; **131** Corbis/ Bettmann; **132c** Getty Images/Bentley Archive/Popperfoto; **132-133** Corbis/Sam Forencich/Solus-Veer; **133t** Topfoto/Charles Walker; **134** The Bridgeman Art Library/Private Collection/Look and Learn; **135t** Mary Evans Picture Library; **135b** DK Images; **137t** Corbis/Lindsay Hebberd; **137b** Topfoto/Fortean.

Illustrators
Pages: 1, 88 © Danny Staten; **6-7, 63, 90** Paul Robinson; **8-9, 20-21, 22l, 28-29, 44-45, 57-58, 72-73, 86-87, 98-99, 112-113, 114-115 124-125** Gill Tomblin; **55t**© Elsa Godfrey; **71r** Johnny McMonagle; **79** Jane Laurie; **81t** Ashley Nagy; **123** © Yuri Leitch; **136** © Bob Eggleton